SOME AUTHENTIC ACTS OF THE EARLY MARTYRS

Oxford University Press

London   Edinburgh   Glasgow   Copenhagen
New York   Toronto   Melbourne   Capetown
Bombay   Calcutta   Madras   Shanghai
Humphrey Milford Publisher to the UNIVERSITY

INSCRIPTION OVER THE TOMB OF SS. PERPETUA AND FELICITAS
DISCOVERED IN THE BASILICA MAIORUM, AT CARTHAGE

See note, p. 10

SOME AUTHENTIC ACTS OF THE EARLY MARTYRS

TRANSLATED WITH NOTES AND
INTRODUCTIONS BY

E. C. E. OWEN

LATE ASSISTANT MASTER IN HARROW SCHOOL
SOMETIME FELLOW OF NEW COLLEGE, OXFORD

LONDON
SOCIETY FOR PROMOTING
CHRISTIAN KNOWLEDGE
NORTHUMBERLAND AVENUE W.C. 2

Published by The Clarendon Press, 1927.

Transferred to S.P.C.K., 1933.

CUTHBERTO H. TURNER

LL.D., D.LITT.

Sacrae Scripturae Exegeseos apud
Oxonienses Professori

VIRO CUM IN THEOLOGIA TUM IN AMICITIA

PRAECLARO

HOC OPUSCULUM

D. D. D.

AMICUS

E. C. E. OWEN

PREFACE

THIS translation is guided by two principles : (1) I have tried to keep the simplicity which characterizes the greater part of these Acts, even at the cost of some harshness. In the *Passion of SS. Perpetua and Felicitas* to reduce all to a uniform smoothness would be to obliterate distinction of authorship as well as of style. (2) In vocabulary I have taken the Authorized Version of the Bible as my model. This was almost inevitable from the number of New Testament quotations, phrases, and distinctive words imbedded in the text, but in any case I should have chosen it as most suitable to the matter in hand. At the same time I have avoided pronounced archaisms as well as the use (except occasionally for clearness) of ' thou ' and ' thee ', for the scene is usually laid in the ordinary courts of law, and the style is seldom consciously heightened, serious but familiar.

I have special obligations to acknowledge to the Very Rev. J. Armitage Robinson, Dean of Wells, who has most kindly allowed me to borrow largely from the introduction and notes to his edition of the *Passion of SS. Perpetua and Felicitas* and his *Acts of the Scillitan Martyrs,* and to use the texts ; to the *Dix Leçons sur les Martyrs* of M. Paul Allard and an article of his in *Revue des Quest. Hist.,* vol. 49 (1913); to *Les Actes des Martyrs* of M. Edmond Le Blant, and also to his *Étude sur les Sarcophages chrétiens, Inscriptions chrétiennes de la Gaule,* as well as to an article by him in *Revue de l'Art Chrétien,* vol. xxi, 1876; to the *Legends of the Saints* (Eng. trans.) by Père Delehaye, S. J. ; to

Herr D. Rudolf Knopf's *Ausgewählte Märtyrerakten*, from which my text is usually taken; to the Rev. B. J. Kidd's *History of the Church to A.D. 461*; to the Rev. F. J. Foakes Jackson's *History of the Christian Church to A.D. 461*; to Herr O. von Gebhardt's *Acta Martyrum*; to Herr P. B. Gams' *Die Kirchengeschichte von Spanien*; to Messrs. Harris and Gifford's *Acts of S. Perpetua* (referred to as H. in the notes); to articles by Signor P. Franchi de' Cavalieri in *Römische Quartalschrift* (1898), and by Mr. J. W. Thompson in *American Journal of Theology* in 1912 and 1913; to Herr Th. Mommsen's articles in *Expositor*, 1890, and in *Texte und Unters.*, vol. iii. I have also occasionally consulted the Rev. A. J. Mason's *The Historic Martyrs of the Primitive Church*, the Rev. H. M. Gwatkin's *Selections from Early Writers, illustrative of Church History*, and Mr. T. H. Bindley's *Translation of the Epistle of the Gallican Churches*, and received valuable help from them in the solution of difficult passages. I have to thank the Warden of Wadham, Prof. C. H. Turner, the Rev. Dom R. H. Connolly, O.S.B., the Rev. Charles Harris, D.D., and the Rev. Charles Plummer, C.C.C., Oxford, for kind help and valuable suggestions. My obligations to writers of the past such as M. Th. Ruinart and Bishop Lightfoot are too numerous to acknowledge by name. The Index is the work of my wife.

E. C. E. O.

5 *March* 1927.

ERRATA

Page 54, line 9 from bottom, *for* Andronica *read* Agathonica

95, line 22, *for* Valerius *read* Valerian

98, line 32, *for* Julianus and Julianus *read* Julian and Julian

102, line 21, *for* Son *read* son

150, line 22, *for* Passion *read* burial

173, col. 1, line 19, *for* Limbs *read* Limbo

col. 2, line 16, *for* μυστήριον *read* μυστήριον

180, col. 1, line 20, *delete* 143

col. 2, *after* Valerian the younger (Caesar) *insert* Valerian (Martyr), 143

Owen: Christian Martyrs, facing p. 8

CONTENTS

NOTE ON THE FRONTISPIECE

'HERE ARE THE MARTYRS SATURUS, SATURNINUS, REVOCATUS, SECUNDULUS, FELICITAS, PERPETUA, WHO SUFFERED ON THE NONES (7th) OF MARCH'

In 1907 Père A. L. Delattre of the Musée Lavigerie at Carthage, to whose great kindness I owe this photograph, discovered and pieced together this inscription over the tomb of SS. Perpetua and Felicitas and their companions (p. 74). It was discovered in the Basilica Maiorum at Carthage, in which Victor Vitensis, an African bishop of the fifth century who had seen the place, says 'the bodies of SS. Perpetua and Felicitas were buried' (*Hist. Vand., Pers.* i. 3). First come the names of the men in the order of their deaths, but Secundulus last because he died before the fight with the beasts (p. 87), then the women similarly ordered, the slave Felicitas before the noble Perpetua.

GENERAL INTRODUCTION

'BY the reading of these (the *Acts of Polycarp* and other ancient martyrdoms) the hearts of the devout are so affected that they can never have enough of them: that this is so each can verify in accordance with his own capacity and experience. Certainly I have never seen anything in Church history, the reading of which leaves me more deeply moved, so that I seem to be transported beyond myself' ('ut non amplius meus esse videar') J. J. Scaliger, *an. Eus.* 2183 (quoted by Jacobson, *Patr. Ap.* ii. 604). The emotion expressed in these memorable words of the great Scaliger will be shared by all who read the Acts of the martyrs with an open mind. But that they may do this, certain prejudices must be overcome. The first and most *Authen-* serious of these results from the impression that the records *ticity* of martyrdom are full of absurd miracles and unreal *of Acts.* pietism and are generally untrustworthy. To remove this we must distinguish between authentic and unauthentic Acts.

The Bollandist Père H. Delehaye, S. J. (*Legends of the Saints*, Eng. trans., p. 111 foll.) divides the Acts of the martyrs and other documents dealing with martyrdom into six classes:

(1) Official reports from the archives of the governor, or other judge, who tried the case. In certain acts nothing is added to these except such commentary and connecting passages as may make out of the official report a narrative of the martyrdom. These, whether authentic or constructed after this pattern, are properly called *Acta*: the rest, i. e. simple narratives written by Christians, are known as *Passiones* (Lat.) or *Martyria* (Gk.).

(2) Accounts of eyewitnesses.

(3) Accounts, of which the *principal* source is a *written*

document belonging to one or other of the preceding classes, e. g. the *Martyrdom of S. Pionius.*

(4) Acts of which the source is not a written document, but the fantastic combination of a few real events in a framework of pure imagination, in other words *historical romances,* e. g. *S. Felicitas and her Seven Sons.*

(5) *Imaginative romances* in which the *hero* himself is the creation of the poet. The well-known history of SS. Barlaam and Joasaph belongs to this class.

(6) Forgeries intended to deceive the reader, such as the apostolic legends of France.

This classification is approved by Harnack, and Bardenhewer's in *Geschichte der altkirchlichen Literatur,* ii. 664–97, is much the same, except that the latter makes one of Delehaye's first two classes.

Scholars are generally agreed about the Acts to be placed in the first two classes. Delehaye gives twelve, Bardenhewer thirty-three, by promoting some of Delehaye's third class. To these authentic records should be added a number of accounts of martyrdoms in Christian writers of recognized credibility such as Eusebius, who wrote two books on the martyrs (*a*) *On the Ancient Martyrs,* which is lost, (*b*) *On the Martyrs of Palestine,* describing the persecution of Diocletian there, of which he, as Bishop of Caesarea, was an eyewitness, besides notices in his *Ecclesiastical History.* Other such writers are Prudentius, S. Chrysostom, S. Basil, S. Augustine, the historian Socrates, &c.

The martyrdoms translated in my book come, except those of SS. *Carpus, Papylus and Agathonica,* and *S. Marinus,* from Delehaye's classes (1) and (2), and, except that of *S. Procopius,* are also in Bardenhewer's first class. The *Acts of S. Carpus* are vouched for by Harnack, *Text. und Unt.,* Bd. iii, p. 435 foll., and by Bardenhewer, and *the Martyrdom of S. Marinus* comes from Eusebius, *Eccl. Hist.* vii. 15. So the reader can put complete confidence in their trustworthiness.

It will be asked what are the marks of authenticity. These are *external*, such as quotation by early and good authors, and *internal*, which, speaking generally, are historical accuracy of date, &c., truth to the ascertained procedure in the ascertained order, the correct use of technical terms, absence as a whole of the miraculous (Le Blant, pp. 37, 96–7; Delehaye, p. 77; Ruinart, *Act. Mart. pref.* i. 7), and of extravagant features such as prolonged and wordy altercation between the prisoner and the judge (Robinson, *Passion of S. Perpetua, Texts and Studies*, i. 2, p. 15), and dramatic propriety. Instances of the first four can be found by the reader himself in the text and notes, but something more may be said of the miraculous and of what I have called dramatic propriety.

Characteristics of authentic Acts.

The remarks of Le Blant (*Les Actes des Martyrs*, p. 37), a scholar unsurpassed in martyrology, are worth quoting; 'When found in the Acts of the martyrs these marks (of the miraculous) should create a doubt of their antiquity: nothing of the sort indeed appears in Christian texts of the first order. . . . There are no miracles in these documents other than those of a fearless and profound faith'. A few examples may be given of this intrusion of the marvellous into later texts. Elizabeth of Hungary laid in the bed which she shared with her husband a leper, whom no one else would touch. The indignant duke rushed into the room and tore off the bedclothes. 'But at that instant God Almighty opened the eyes *of his soul* (" Tunc aperuit Deus *interiores* principis oculos "), and instead of a leper he saw the figure of Christ crucified stretched upon the bed.' Later hagiographers, dissatisfied with the noble simplicity of the historian's words, wrote in their place, 'There lay a bleeding crucifix with outstretched arms' (Delehaye, p. 90). Nothing can be more sober and unadorned than the account of the martyrdom of S. Procopius (p. 127). There are three main versions of the legend

Miracles and other extravagant features.

which developed from it. The earliest, though the writer had in his hands the simple narrative given here, describes S. Procopius as overwhelming the judge with reproaches and insults, and quoting in a long speech not only Homer (v. p. 128), but Plato, Aristotle, Socrates, Hermes Trismegistus, and others. He is repeatedly tortured in the most horrible ways, his wounds are healed in an instant, and the executioner sent to cut off his head is paralysed and falls down dead. It is not necessary to go through all his changes in the second and third versions of the legend. In the second, among other remarkable additions, the old Reader is turned into a Duke of Alexandria and puts to flight an army of 6,000 with his miraculous Cross. Not the history of S. Procopius only, but those of S. Polycarp and S. Perpetua illustrate in certain small points the growth of the miraculous or extravagant element. In the *Martyrdom of S. Polycarp*, ch. xvi, we find in the later texts (v. note p. 39) ' then issued forth a dove and a stream of blood ', where the earlier texts have only ' a stream of blood '. In the short Latin version of the *Passion of S. Perpetua* the interrogatory of the original is lengthened and the simplicity spoilt.

Le Blant urged with great learning that even in Acts that are otherwise untrustworthy there are to be found details which are too rare to be invented, and which are often confirmed by authentic Acts, by historians or codes of law. Personally I am convinced that a number of the details he quotes are genuine, but it is difficult to refute Delehaye's contention (*op. cit.*, p. 224) that from such fragments, even if original, it is impossible to reconstruct the true story.

Reasons why authentic Acts are so few. Why, of the immense number of Acts of martyrs, so few authentic acts remain can be accounted for in two ways: (1) By the deliberate efforts made by persecutors to destroy all Christian books. This was particularly marked under Diocletian. Sometimes too a determined attempt was made to prevent any publication of the details of a martyrdom, from fear of the conversions produced thereby. (2) By the preference shown by the writers of the lives of saints for the elaborate and interpolated rather than the simple and original versions. Delehaye notes (p. 78) that ' between a purely historical document and a touched up version, adorned with fantastic developments and interlarded with fables, a mediaeval public rarely hesitated'. There is often a single manuscript of the former kind, many manuscripts of the latter.

On the contrary the reason why there are sometimes preserved, e. g. in the *Acts of S. Cyprian* or the *Acts of the Scillitan Saints*, the actual notes of the trial, is that reports of the proceedings were taken by shorthand-writers (v. *The Acts of S. Marcellus*, ch. iv, p. 123). Copies of these were often sold to the Christians (v. *Acta S. Tarachi*, Ruinart, p. 451, where the price is 200 denarii (about £6)), and preserved with the relics of the martyr (*Acta S. Felicis* (Gerundae), 1). Dom John Chapman, O.S.B., notes in the *Dublin Review*, Jan. 1927, p. 9, that ' Shorthand-writers were more used by the ancients than by the moderns, even since Sir Isaac Pitman ', and the shorthand-writer (' exceptor ', ' notarius ') was a regular official in every court. *Reasons why the actual notes of the trial are preserved.*

In some Acts, where there is opportunity, a striking mark of authenticity is truth of character. It is noted in the Introduction to the *Martyrdom of S. Polycarp* how true is the description of the old bishop there to the character manifested in his life and in his *Epistle to the Philippians*, his insistence on the duty of pity and forgiveness (*Ep. ad Phil.* ii, v, vi, viii, xii, compared with *Mart.* vii, x), his love of prayer (*Ep. ad Phil.* xii, compared with *Mart.* vii, viii, xiv). A more striking instance is found in the presentation of S. Justin in his *Acts*. Few though his words there are, they have the touch of precision, one might almost say ' donnishness ', characteristic of a *Dramatic propriety.*

philosopher. This came home to me as I was translating his
first words in ch. ii. I made five or six attempts, but none
of them satisfied me, each seemed stiffer and more wooden
than the last. Suddenly I realized that the stiffness was
essential, and that if I lost that I should mistranslate the
passage: 'To obey the commands of our Saviour Jesus
Christ is not worthy of blame or condemnation.' His
other answers in this chapter are in the same vein. In
the *Acts of SS. Carpus, Papylus, and Agathonica* Harnack
has noted the contrast between S. Papylus and S. Carpus,
Papylus taciturn, Carpus talkative, even at the stake.
Again no one can mistake the character of S. Cyprian in the
Acts of his martyrdom. He is a bishop of the Church,
but he is no less a noble, the equal in rank of the proconsul
who is trying him. And the proconsul knows and feels it
too, and 'with difficulty' ('aegre', ch. iv) pronounces
sentence. The night's lodging 'in gentle custody' ('custo-
dia delicata', ch. ii, and *Life of Cyprian* by Pontius,
ch. xv) in the house of an officer of the staff 'with guests
and friends after his custom (*ib.*)', the rich cloak and the
dalmatic which he puts off before the stroke of the sword,
the largesse of twenty-five golden pieces to the executioner
(*Acts*, ch. v) touch the same note of a gallant gentleman,
who 'bears gaiety in his face, and courage in his heart'
(*Life*, xv). There is characteristic brevity too about the replies of the soldier S. Marcellus (p. 123). He makes answer
in single words, as he might at a court-martial, 'I spoke.'
'I served.' 'I spoke.' 'I flung away.' But the most
remarkable examples occur in the *Passion of SS. Perpetua and Felicitas*. The Dean of Wells has shown in great
detail and with much insight (v. p. 74-5) by what fine and
delicate touches the style of S. Perpetua is differentiated
from that of S. Saturus and both from that of the editor.

The ordinary English reader is often subject to another
prejudice. Starting with a national dislike to anything

excessive or demonstrative in religion, and having heard that good emperors, such as Trajan or Marcus Aurelius, were persecutors, he leaps at the suggestion that the Christians were to blame. Only the other day I read an article on Eusebius by one of our most distinguished men of letters which was full of gross mistakes, due partly to ignorance but largely to this form of prejudice. It is a matter, therefore, of great importance to discover (1) what were the causes of the persecution of the Christians, (2) what was the behaviour of Christians as citizens, (3) what was their attitude towards martyrdom.

We may dismiss in a few words allegations which had clearly no foundation. Nero's charge that the Christians had set fire to Rome was obviously meant to avert suspicion from himself, and is given little credit by Tacitus (*Ann.* xv. 44) in spite of his hatred and contempt for the Christians. The charge made in the first and second centuries, as for instance at Lyons (Eus. *H. E.* v. 1, 14, p. 58-9), of 'Thyestean banquets and Oedipodean unions', was disbelieved even as early as the days of Pliny (*Ep.* x. 96), and soon dropped out of sight, till it was revived in the last desperate propaganda of Maximin (A.D. 311). *Causes of persecution of Christians. False charges.*

What the main accusation was is clear from the procedure in court. The accused Christian was required to sacrifice to the genius of the Emperor, sometimes also, as by Pliny and the governor who tried S. Polycarp (ch. ix), to curse Christ. The persecution was for 'the Name' alone. Tertullian complains of this (*Apol.* ii), 'The only thing needed to satisfy the general hatred is, not the investigation of a charge, but the confession of the Name.' What was so remarkable about the trial of a Christian was that he condemned himself. He had only to offer the pinch of incense, and he was free. At Lyons indeed (Eus. *H. E.* i. 5, 33, p. 62 and note) the apostates suffered with the faithful, but this, like other actions of this governor, was *Persecution for 'the Name'.*

illegal, and was only palliated by the complication of other charges. ' Why then ', it will be asked, ' was the Jewish religion, which also forbade sacrifice to the Emperor, an " allowed religion " (" religio licita "), and the Christian banned ? ' The reason is not far to seek. The Jewish was a national religion, and made little or no efforts to obtain converts. It was indeed a liberal act of the Roman Government to tolerate the Jewish refusal, but it involved them in no danger. Far otherwise was it with the Christian religion. Even by Pliny's time (*c.* A.D. 112) it had made such progress in Bithynia that there were ' many (Christians) of all ages; all ranks; and of both sexes ' . . . the temples had been almost deserted, and the public worship had long ceased (*Ep.* x. 96). Tertullian says eighty-five years later : 'We are of·yesterday, yet we have filled all that is yours, cities, islands, villages, free towns, market towns, the camp itself, tribes, town-councils, the palace, the senate, the forum; we have left you your temples alone. . . . If we abandoned you for some far country you would shudder at your solitude, at the silence, the stupor of a dead world ' (*Apol.* 37). More than this, as early as A.D. 95 among the converts were Domitilla, a granddaughter of the Emperor Vespasian, and her husband and cousin Flavius Clemens, an ex-consul. She was banished to an island, he was executed (Dion Cass. lxvii. 14). The noble family of the Acilii, whose first convert and martyr was Acilius Glabrio, consul in 91 (Suet. *Dom.* x), remained Christian; and their tombs may be seen in the catacomb of Priscilla. It is practically certain that even as early as 58 Pomponia Graecina, the wife of Aulus Plautius, the conqueror of Britain, who was ' accused of a foreign superstition ' (Tac. *Ann.* xiii. 32), was a Christian. The ' household of Caesar ' (Phil. iv. 22) was so full of Christian slaves and freedmen at the beginning of the reign of Valerian, that it was ' like a Church ' (Eus. *H. E.* vii. 10).

It is not unnatural that there should have been con-
sternation in government circles, when it is remembered
that the worship of the Emperor's genius was, at all events
in the Provinces, the chief bond of Empire, and that
refusal to sacrifice must have seemed in the eyes of subject
races an insult to the flag as well as an act of sacrilege. The
rulers of India can understand how imperative it must
have appeared to the Government to stop the advance of
Christianity at all costs.

This, though the chief, was not the only charge against *The be-*
the Christians. They were accused of atheism because *haviour of*
they offered no visible sacrifices (Min. Felix, *Oct.* viii). *Christians*
There was a third indictment which, though not sufficient *as citizens.*
to condemn, was capable of creating a strong prejudice
against them. It is this charge which was revived in the
article referred to above, and which is the only living
charge to-day. It was summed up by the Romans as 'odium
humani generis ' and ' inertia '; they were accused, that is
of hostility to the Roman civilization, which was a whole,
and had to be accepted as a whole (Allard, *Dix Leçons*,
p. 126), of taking no share in public, or in the ceremonious
part of private life, of being ' inactive', and consequently
useless, citizens. So far as this was true it was not their
fault. They were not disloyal, they obeyed the Government in all lawful things, they prayed for the Emperor's
safety (*Mart. S. Polyc.* x, *S. Cyp.* i. 2). But, as all officials had
to begin their tenure of office by sacrifice, they could not serve
even on a town-council without being false to their religion;
they could not attend festivals, public or private, which
were celebrated with sacrifice, nor the cruel shows of the
amphitheatre, which were an offence to Christian morality.

In time the pagans themselves realized this, and often
the obligation of sacrifice was relaxed. A Christian would
take the oath of allegiance, and the sacrifice would be
offered, but not by his hand. Eusebius (*H. E.* viii. 1, 2)

tells us that Diocletian appointed several Christians to be provincial governors, at the same time dispensing them from sacrificial duties to which they conscientiously objected (Allard, *ib.*, p. 202). Even the rigorist Tertullian (*De idol.* xvi) countenances attendance at a pagan festival if the Christian has accepted the invitation for some other reason than the sacrifice: he then becomes 'merely a spectator'. Such concessions were bound to be made when, as in many towns in Roman Asia, the whole population had by 311 become Christian (v. Rufinus, *H. E.* ix. 6). When the great persecutions of Decius, Valerian, and Diocletian broke out, they upset a 'modus vivendi' which had already obtained between Christian and pagan, and this increased the horror of the situation.

Christians and military service. In particular it is often alleged, as in the article above-mentioned, that the Christians evaded military service. That is a charge more often brought now than then. As a matter of fact the military oath was not as a rule accompanied by sacrifice, so that a Christian could serve in the army with a clear conscience. The fact that the Thundering Legion was said at the time when the miracle was alleged to have taken place (A. D. 174) to have consisted entirely of Christians shows, whatever may be the truth of the story, that the profession of a soldier was beyond question open to a Christian. Our own short list of thirteen martyrdoms contains the names of two soldiers, SS. Marinus and Marcellus, and Marcellus does not throw up his commission till he is called upon to sacrifice at the celebration of the Emperor's birthday. It is true that some fanatics, especially Montanists such as Tertullian in his later days, regarded, like our Quakers, military service as incompatible with the profession of a Christian. But this attitude was strongly discouraged by the authorities of the Church, and even Tertullian says (*Apol.* 37): 'We are not Brahmins or Indian fakirs. We serve in the army by your side.'

Incidental, but very important, causes of persecution were the whims and quarrels of Emperors, cupidity, and the desire of a scapegoat.

Incidental causes of persecution.

The chief purpose of Ruinart's preface to his *Acta Martyrum* is to maintain as against Dr. H. Dodwell that the number of those martyred was very great. Dr. Dodwell's object was largely controversial, to prove that ' lazy monks ' had exaggerated the number for their own purposes. Few would now think it to be in the interest of any part of the Church to diminish the number of those glorious witnesses who sealed their faith with their blood. That some martyrdoms are fictitious is true. Sometimes this occurs through an error in interpretation. There is a curious example of this in the record of the Martyrs of Lyons (Eus. *H. E.* v. 1. 9), where the name of Zacharias, the father of S. John the Baptist, was taken to be the name of one of the martyrs and added to the list. Sometimes it is due to ignorance of another kind, as in the famous case of S. Philomena in 1802. The number of these, however, is inconsiderable. But it is an object of great interest to estimate roughly, for no accurate figures are obtainable, the numbers of the martyrs.

Number of the Martyrs.

In the first two centuries the number of martyrs was relatively small, but, as Harnack says, ' over the head of every Christian hung the sword of Damocles.' And in the persecution of Nero at all events numbers perished, ' a great multitude,' says Tacitus (*Ann.* xv. 44). Much has been made of the words of Origen (*c. Cels.* iii. 8) in 249: ' A few at intervals, easily counted, have died for the Christian faith.' But it must be remembered (1) that Origen was writing before the great and systematic persecutions of Decius, Valerian, and Diocletian; (2) that he is dwelling in this passage on the kindness of God who would not suffer ' the whole Christian people to perish ', and that in another passage he speaks of the martyrs as ' many '

(v. Ruinart, *Pref.* ii. 22). St. Dionysius, under Decius, (Eus. *H.E.* vi. 42; vii. 11, 20) writes of ' men and women, young and old, young girls and old women, soldiers and civilians, persons of every rank and age winning the crown of martyrdom under the lash, by fire or by the sword '. For Valerian we have among other testimonies that of the *Passion of SS. James and Marian*, ch. xii, which shows that at a single place on a single day great numbers suffered. For Diocletian (303-13) we possess the contemporaneous account of Eusebius, though he deals only with the East. He estimates that 10,000 men, not counting women and children, perished in Egypt alone. In Nicomedia ' a dense multitude ' (πλῆθος ἄθρουν) were beheaded (*H. E.* viii. 6. 6), others burnt, ' another multitude ' thrown into the sea. He himself saw with his own eyes (*ib.* viii. 9, 3–4) ' a great number perish on one day, some by sword, others by fire. The swords were blunted or broken, the executioners worn out, so that frequent relays were necessary '. He tells us (*H.E.* viii. 11), and he is borne out by Lactantius (*Div. Inst.* v. 11), that, when a certain town in Phrygia was invested, the inhabitants were called upon to sacrifice. They refused to a man, declaring themselves to be Christians. They were then driven into the church and burnt alive from the magistrates to the humblest citizen. Other evidence in plenty may be read in Allard (*Dix leçons*, pp. 134–50), but perhaps the most impressive testimony is provided by the long lines of martyrs' graves in the catacombs of Rome.

We may now turn to the Acts of the Martyrs themselves, authentic Acts, such as those in this collection. What lessons do they have for us?

Two, to begin with, so obvious that each may be expressed in a sentence, *witness* and *example*.

Martyrs as evidence. ' I readily believe those stories whose witnesses get their throats cut ' (Pascal, *Pensées*, titre 28 (p. 196 ed. 1712)).

' The apostle bids us take part in the remembrance of the *Martyrs* saints because to hold in memory those who with all their *as ex-* hearts lived in faith strengthens those who wish to imitate *amples.* the better part' (*Martyrdom of S. Pionius*, a martyr under Decius, A. D. 250, ch. i).

A third point of interest concerns specially a country *The Evan-* like our own. There are many people, unacquainted with *gelical* Church history, who practically hold, though they might *character* not set it down in black and white, that all the teaching *of the* and practice of the Church from the close of the Apostolic *Acts of the* age to the Reformation was corrupt and without value to *Martyrs.* an Evangelical Christian. Others have no such prejudice, but are almost completely ignorant of the history of the second and third centuries. Nothing will give men and women belonging to either of these classes so vivid a picture, in such brief compass, of the beauty of those early days as the authentic Acts of the Martyrs. In particular they will learn how truly evangelical their belief and practice were. This is obvious on every page, but I may point out one or two striking pieces of evidence.

The Acts are full of quotations from the New Testament. It is very remarkable that at a time when the Canon had only just been fixed (end of second century), or was still uncertain, there is hardly one definite reference to those books outside the Canon which were at first ranked with the New Testament Scriptures, such as the *Epistle of Barnabas*, *The Shepherd* of Hermas, the *Epistle to the Corinthians* of S. Clement. There may be, as the Dean of Wells believes, reminiscences of *The Shepherd* and other uncanonical books in S. Perpetua's visions. But the Canonical books are not only quoted continually, and all alike with scarcely an exception, Jude, the Pastoral Epistles, and 2 Peter, but the whole narrative of the Acts is coloured by their characteristic words. The Acts of the Martyrs of Lyons are a very cento of such words and phrases, e. g. i. 6, 48–9; ii. 5. Among the evangelical beliefs most emphasized are the union of Christ with believers which gave them their supernatural fortitude (*Letter of the Churches of Vienne and Lyons*, Eus. *H. E.* v. 1, 23, *Passion of SS. Perpetua and Felicitas*, xv), and the inspiration of the individual Christian by the Holy Ghost (*S. Perpetua*, passim, but especially chaps. i, xxi fin.). The martyrs follow with exact and literal obedience the commands of Christ and His Apostles, in not seeking martyrdom (S. Matt. x. 23; *Mart. of S. Polycarp*, iv and xix, where Polycarp's martyrdom is said to be 'according to the Gospel'), and praying for their persecutors (*Acts of S. Marcellus*, v; *Epistle of the Churches of Vienne and Lyons* v. 2, 5; Acts vii. 60), and paying honour to those in authority (*Mart. of S. Polycarp*, x; Rom. xiii. 1 and 7; 1 Pet. ii. 13 foll.), and praying for them (*Acts of S. Cyprian*, i. 2; 1 Tim. ii. 1 foll.).

Catholic beliefs and practices. Evangelical believers will find in these Acts a creed as evangelical as their own. They may be surprised to discover united with this beliefs and practices which are unfamiliar, or which they have been accustomed to regard with suspicion. The union of evangelical piety with Catholic beliefs and practices may well give them pause. These latter cannot well be corrupt, the fruit is too good and the times too early. At the date of the first Acts men who have talked with the Apostles are living or have only recently died; the latest are no further removed from them than our grandfathers from the Reformation; the Apostolic tradition is still living. Let me give some of these Catholic beliefs and practices. If we may judge from the *Martyrdom of S. Polycarp*, ix (v. note), Infant Baptism was already practised (A. D. 70). Martyrdom was regarded as a kind of Baptism, 'the Baptism of Blood' (*S. Perpetua* xxi; *Passion of SS. James and Marian*, xi). The deaths, or ' heavenly birthdays', of the martyrs were annually honoured (*Mart. of S. Polycarp*, xviii), and, as we learn elsewhere, the Eucharist was celebrated on altars above their graves, careful distinction being made between the worship due to Christ and the love and remembrance due to the martyrs (*ib.* xvii). Their relics were preserved as ' of more value than precious stones' (*ib.* xvii, xviii), and the brethren spread their handkerchiefs on the ground before S. Cyprian to catch his sacred blood (*Acts of S. Cyprian*, v) ; the smoking ashes were quenched in wine (*Acts of S. Fructuosus*, vi). But those who had carried away to their own homes some of the ashes of S. Fructuosus and his deacons were ordered in a vision to restore them that all the relics might be buried together, and as late as S. Gregory the Great (end of sixth century) any separation of the relics of a saint was strictly forbidden. They heard the confessions of the lapsed and reconciled them (*Ep. of the Churches of Vienne and Lyons* v. 2, 5, where the technical terms are already in use). But it is noticeable that no invocation of martyrs or other saints, even of the Blessed Virgin, is mentioned, though this would be particularly natural in the last moments of the martyrs. There is a vivid sense of Communion with the Saints, as in Origen (*de Or.* xi) ' Not the High Priest (Christ) alone prays with those who pray sincerely, but also the angels . . . as also the souls of the saints who have already fallen asleep ', and supplications to the dead for their remembrance and prayers occur at this date in the Catacombs. The only allusion, I think, to Our Lady in these Acts is in the *Passion of SS. James and Marian*, xiii, where she is mentioned with deep reverence. On the other hand, prayers *for* the dead are in evidence, S. Perpetua prays for her dead brother (ch. vii), and he is released from suffering (ch. viii, v. notes there). Fasting is referred to in the *Acts of S. Fructuosus*, iii (v. note), and the fast before communion in the *Passion of SS. James and Marian*, viii. 1, and the use of technical terms shows that it has been already systematized. The preparation by the Eucharist for martyrdom in the latter passage is advised by the contemporary S. Cyprian (*Ep*. liv, §§ 1 and 2), ' Fortify them by the protection of the Body and Blood of Jesus Christ.'   There is a mystical passage about the Eucharist in *Pass. S. Perp*. iv (v. note), there, too, mention is made of the ' Great Amen ' which concludes the Prayer of Consecration (cf. *Mart. of S. Polyc*. xv).   The kiss of Peace is spoken of in *Pass. S. Perp*. xii and xxi.   The devotion to ' Mother' Church (*Ep. of the Churches of Vienne and Lyons* v. 2, 6–7) is very marked.   She is called the ' Virgin Mother' (*ib*. v. 1, 45), and in *Acts of S. Fruct*. iii, there is a reference to the ' Catholic Church ', which is probably a quotation from the Mozarabic Liturgy (v. note).   There is a peculiar reverence shown to the person of the Bishop (v. *Mart. of S. Polyc*. xiii; *Ep. of the Churches of Vienne and Lyons* v. 1, 29–31; *Acts of S. Cyprian*, v; *Acts of S. Fruct*. iii).

So much for these ancient Acts and their mysterious beauty.   If we are inclined to feel that they belong to another world than ours, and can have no bearing on our lives, we may do well to read an article of M. E. Le Blant (*Revue de l'Art Chrétien*, 1876, vol. xxi) on the Christian martyrs in China.   We shall find there the old calumnies, more than all the old tortures, the old faith and courage; ' He goes to death as to a feast ' was said of one of them in the last century (cf. *Pass. S. Perp*. xviii).   We shall do well also to remember the tens of thousands of Russian and Greek Asiatic Christians of the Orthodox Church who have been martyred in the last ten years. ' The blood of the martyrs is ' still ' the seed of the Church '—' Si vetera fidei exempla, et Dei gratiam testificantia et aedificationem hominis operantia, propterea in litteris sunt digesta, ut lectione eorum quasi repraesentatione rerum et Deus honoretur et homo confortetur; cur non et nova documenta aeque utrique causae convenientia et digerantur ' (*Pass. S. Perp*. i. init.)?

SUMMARY OF THE PERSECUTIONS IN THE ROMAN EMPIRE

Nero, A. D. 54–68.   Persecution 64–8, SS. Peter and Paul martyred at Rome (S. Clement of Rome *ad Cor*. v.), with a 'huge multitude' (Tac. *Ann.* xv. 44), who were burnt and otherwise tortured (Juv. i. 155), on the pretext that they had set fire to Rome.

Galba, Otho, Vitellius, 68–9.

Vespasian, 69–79.

Titus, 79–81.

Domitian, 81–96.   A number put to death under charge of ' atheism ', among them Flavius Clemens, consul and cousin of the Emperor, his wife Domitilla, and Acilius Glabrio, ex-consul.

Nerva, 96–8.

Trajan, 98–117.   In *c.* 112 instructed Pliny the Younger, governor of Bithynia (*Letters of Pliny and Trajan*, x. 96) that :

   (1) Christians were not to be sought out, and anonymous accusations were to be neglected :

   (2) Those who were regularly accused and acknowledged themselves Christians were to be punished :

   (3) Those who had said they had never been Christians or had ceased to be Christians, and proved it by sacrificing were to be pardoned.

   This rescript guided the procedure against Christians for a century till Septimius Severus.   Chief martyr S. Ignatius, Bishop of Antioch.

Hadrian, 117–38.   A. D. 124 in a rescript to Minucius Fundanus, governor of Asia, repeated provisions (1) and (2) of Trajan's rescript.   A reign of comparative peace.

Antoninus Pius, 138–61.   Repeated provisions (1) and (2) of Trajan's rescript in rescripts to cities of Macedonia, Thessaly, and Greece.   Chief martyr S. Polycarp, Bishop of Smyrna (p. 31).

Marcus Aurelius, 161–80.   Repeated provision (3) of Trajan's rescript, v. Martyrs of Lyons, i. 47 (p. 65).   Among the martyrs were SS. Carpus, Papylus and Agathonica (p. 42), SS. Justin and his companions (p. 47), the Scillitan Martyrs (p. 71), the Martyrs of Lyons (p. 53).

Commodus, 180–92.   } Almost complete peace from per-
Pertinax, Didius Julianus, 193. }   secution.

Septimius Severus, 193–211. A new era began. From this time onwards (a) persecution was regulated by a series of new edicts, (b) Christians were not accused by private prosecutor, but *sought out by the state*.

Under Septimius Severus the newly converted and their converters were punished, not the old Christians.

Martyrs SS. Saturus and his pupils Perpetua and Felicitas and their companions (p. 74).

Geta and Caracalla, 211–17. Same policy.

Macrinus, 217–18.   ⎫
Heliogabalus, 218–22.   ⎬   No persecution.
Alexander Severus, 222–35. ⎭

Maximin the Thracian, 235–37. Persecution against leaders, but extended to others by mob-violence and the cruelty of certain governors.

The two Gordians, 237–8.   ⎫
Gordianus III, 238–44.   ⎬   No persecution.
Philip the Arabian, 244–9. ⎭

Decius, 249–51. By the edict of 250 certificates of sacrifice demanded of all Christians in town and country. Punishment exile with confiscation of goods ; torture and imprisonment used to induce repentance ; death seldom inflicted ; persecution world-wide. Many of the martyrs were bishops, such as S. Fabian, of Rome.

Gallus, 251–2. Issued a new edict to compel the Christians to sacrifice.

Volusian, 252.

Aemilian, 253.

Valerian, 253–60. Peace restored till 257, when first edict of persecution ordered bishops and priests to worship the gods, and forbade Christians under pain of death to frequent the cemeteries or hold meetings for worship (pp. 96, 105) ; second edict in 258 ordered that (a) bishops, priests and deacons who refused to sacrifice should be put to death at once ; (b) Christians of noble birth should have their property confiscated (having lost the privileges of noble birth by the loss of fortune, men were punished with death, women with exile) ; (c) the Caesariani (slaves and freedmen of the imperial house) should lose their property, and be made slaves of the soil. Under (a) suffered among others Pope S. Sixtus ii. and his deacons, S. Cyprian (p. 93), SS. Fructuosus and his deacons (p. 100), SS. James and Marian (p. 105), under (b) S. Aemilian (p. 113).

Gallienus, 260–8. Granted cemeteries and other places of worship to the Church. Yet isolated martyrdoms occurred, e. g. of

S. Marinus (p. 119), owing to the confusion of the time (Age of the Thirty Tyrants).

Claudius II, 268–70.

Aurelian, 270–5. Issued new edict of persecution, but died before it had effect.

Tacitus, 275–6.

Probus, 276–82.

Carus, 282–3.

Carinus and Numerian, 283–4.

Diocletian alone, 284–6.

Diocletian and Maximian, 286–92.

Diocletian and Maximian *Augusti*; Constantius and Galerius *Caesars*, 292–304. In 303 (the army had before this been purged of Christians) Diocletian, under influence of Maximian, issued first edict—that churches should be destroyed, sacred Scriptures burnt, Christians of position should lose their honours, and those of lower rank their liberty. Death was not pronounced as penalty, but many died.

Second edict that leaders of Christians should be thrown into prison.

Third edict that imprisoned clergy who refused to sacrifice should suffer the most cruel tortures.

Fourth edict 304 that all Christians everywhere in town and country should offer sacrifice or be put to death, a war of extermination.

Constantius and Galerius *Augusti*; Severus and Maximin Daza *Caesars*, 305. After abdication of Diocletian and Maximian (May 1, 305) persecution (which had already ceased in western Europe) still continued in eastern Europe, Province of Asia, and Egypt, which were under government of Galerius and Maximin Daza.

Fifth edict 306 in the same quarters in the same terms as that of 304.

Sixth edict 308 in the same quarters to force idolatry on Christians, by sprinkling all articles sold with lustral water, and compelling all who visited the baths to sacrifice.

Galerius; Maximin Daza; Constantine (already Caesar, 306); Licinius; Maximian (restd); Maxentius, 307–13. In 311 Galerius (in union with Constantine and Licinius), ill of the same disease as Herod (Acts xii. 23), the ‘tyrant’s disease’, granted toleration to the Christians, and asked for their prayers.

Among the martyrs of this persecution were S. Marcellus (p. 121) and S. Cassian (p. 125) in 298 in the preliminary attack on

Christian soldiers, and S. Procopius (p. 127) under the first edict of 303.

Maximin Daza renewed the persecution after Galerius's death (311), having prepared for it by a campaign of calumny and the setting up of a rival hierarchy.

In March 313 Constantine and his colleague Licinius, their rivals being dead or conquered, gave complete freedom to the Christians by the Edict of Milan. Here the era of persecution ended except for a few months in the East under Licinius in 323, and the latter part of the Pagan Revival under Julian the Apostate, 361–3.

P.S. It is uncertain under what law Christians were liable to punishment. The first edict against them in 112 simply regulated a previously existing law. There are two views :

(1) that of Allard (*Dix leçons sur les Martyrs*, pp. 87, 92), that the Name alone was punishable in accordance with what Eusebius (*H.E.* v. 21) calls the ἀρχαῖος νόμος, the 'ancient law', which Tertullian (*Apol.* v. and *ad nat.* i. 7) attributes to Nero. It may have taken the simple form found in documents of the time *Christiani non sint*, lit. ' Christians must not exist.'

(2) That of Mommsen (*Der Religionsfrevel nach römischen Recht* in *Hist. Zeitschrift 1890*, vol. lxiv, pp. 389–429, and *Christianity in the Roman Empire* in *Expositor*, vol. viii), that they were charged nominally under the Lex Maiestatis (*Law of Treason*) for refusing the religious honours due to the Emperor, but practically under the vague power, known as *coercitio*, or coercion, which entitled prefects, governors, and other high officials to act summarily against persons thought to be dangerous. It is an objection to this view that it is precisely such vague powers that Trajan in his edict condemned, *conquirendi non sunt*, ' They must not be sought out,' though he entertained no doubt that Christians were punishable as such.

I

MARTYRDOM OF S. POLYCARP (A. D. 155–6)

S. Polycarp was Bishop of Smyrna, a disciple of S. John, appointed by him according to Tertullian (*de Praescr*. xxxii) as bishop in charge of the Church at Smyrna. It was to him possibly (*Chron. Pasch.*, p. 470, A. D. 101) that S. John committed the charge of the young man, who afterwards fell away, and became a robber, and was finally restored to the Church by the Apostle. S. Irenaeus (v. p. 53), the great Bishop of Lyons, himself a disciple of S. Polycarp, speaks of him (*Haer*. iii. 3) as one who ' had been trained by the Apostles, and had conversed with many who had seen Christ '. ' He would describe ', the same authority says in another place (Euseb. *Hist. Eccl.* v. 20), ' his intercourse with John and with the rest of those who had seen the Lord, and would relate their words. And whatsoever things he had heard from these about the Lord and about His miracles and about His teaching, Polycarp, as having received them from eyewitnesses of the life of the Word, would relate them altogether in accordance with the Scriptures.' Thus, as the last representative of those who had known the Apostles, and of ' those who had seen the Lord ', he was held in the greatest reverence throughout the Christian world. S. Ignatius, Bishop of Antioch, himself also a hearer of the Apostles, stayed with him on his way to his martyrdom at Rome (A. D. 110), and after he left Smyrna wrote letters to S. Polycarp and to the Church at Smyrna, urging the dispatch of messengers to sustain the Church at Antioch. In A. D. 154, just before his martyrdom, S. Polycarp visited Rome to discuss with the Roman Church certain questions, especially concerning the date of Easter, about which it was at variance with the Churches of Asia. They came to no agreement, but Pope Anicetus treated him with high honour and they parted in peace. While there he met the heretic Marcion. ' Do you recognize me ? ' said Marcion. ' Yes,' replied Polycarp, ' I recognize the first-born of Satan.'

Except for a few fragments the only writing of S. Polycarp we possess is the *Epistle to the Philippians*, sent in answer to their request for copies of any of the letters written by S. Ignatius. This letter recalls (Foakes Jackson, *Hist. of the Chr. Ch.*, p. 120) the language of S. Peter rather than of S. John. It is full of practical directions about deacons, priests, widows, maidens, young men, recalling 1 Tim. iii. and v, about covetousness, charity to the erring, and especially about prayer (ch. xii). The last reminds us of the touching description in his Acts (chaps. v, vii, xiv) of his own persistence in prayer : ' Pray ', he says in his letter, ' for kings and magistrates and leading men, and for those who persecute and hate you, and for the enemies of the Cross, that your fruit may be manifest in all things, that you may be perfect in Him.' Words from the language of the common people occur in the Epistle e. g. ch. ii, μὴ ἀποδιδόντες . . . γρόνθον ἀντὶ γρόνθου, ' not rendering fisticuffs for fisticuffs.' The most notable doctrinal reference is to those Docetists who denied (ch. vii) that Christ had come in the flesh and did not believe in the Resurrection of the Body (cf. Duchesne, *Early Hist. of the Ch.*, Eng. trans., p. 60). The immense respect for him is shown by the fact that the account of his martyrdom was sent not only to the Church at Philomelium but ' to all the dioceses of the Holy Catholic Church in every place '. Lightfoot gives the date as A. D. 155, Prof. C. H. Turner as 156.   *Text from* KNOPF

T HE Church of God which dwells in Smyrna to the Church of God which dwells in Philomelium and to all the dioceses of the Holy Catholic Church in every place. May the mercy, peace, and love of God the Father 5 and of our Lord Jesus Christ be multiplied.

I. 1. We write unto you, brethren, the story of the martyrs and of blessed Polycarp, who put an end to the persecution, setting his seal thereto by his martyrdom. For almost all that went before so happened, that the Lord 10 might show forth anew an example of martyrdom which is conformable to the Gospel. 2. For he waited to be betrayed, as did also the Lord, that we also might be imitators of Him, looking not only on our own things, but also on the things of others. For it is a mark of true and steadfast love to desire not our own salvation only but that of all the brethren.

II. 1. Blessed and noble are all martyrdoms that happen according to the will of God. For we should act with discretion leaving the power over all events to God. 2. For who can fail to admire their nobility and patience and love of their Master? Who being so torn with scourges that the framework of the flesh was laid bare to the veins and arteries within, showed such patience that the very bystanders felt pity and sorrow, while some reached so high a pitch of nobility that no sound or groan escaped them, making manifest to us all that in the hour of their torture the martyrs of Christ were absent from the flesh, or rather that the Lord was present and of their company. 3. Fixing their thoughts on the grace of Christ they despised the torments of the world, redeeming in one hour eternal punishment. And the fire of their inhuman torturers was cold to them, for their eyes were set on escape from the eternal fire which is never quenched, and with the eyes of the heart they looked upon the good things reserved for them that endure, which ear hath not heard, nor eye seen, ' neither have they entered into the heart of man,' but they were revealed by the Lord unto them who were no longer men, but already angels. 4. Likewise those who were condemned to the beasts endured terrible torments, having harrows laid beneath them, and being tormented with other kinds of manifold tortures, that the Devil, if he could, might through the continual torment turn them to deny their faith; for he devised many things against them.

III. 1. But, thanks be to God, he did not prevail against all. For the noble Germanicus gave strength to their cowardice by his own fortitude, who made a notable fight with the beasts. For when the proconsul endeavoured to prevail upon him, bidding him take pity on his own youth, he with violence dragged the wild beast towards him, wishing to be rid the sooner of their life of unrighteousness and sin.

2. At this all the multitude, wondering at the nobility 5 of the people of Christ, who were beloved of God and honoured Him, cried out, ' Away with the Atheists ! Seek Polycarp ! '

IV. But one, Quintus by name, a Phrygian just arrived from Phrygia, lost heart when he saw the beasts. He it was 10 who constrained himself and some others to come forward of their own motion. Him the proconsul after much entreaty persuaded to take the oath and offer sacrifice. Therefore, brethren, we do not commend those who give themselves up; for this is not the teaching of the Gospel.

15 V. 1. The excellent Polycarp, on hearing the news was not dismayed, but wished to remain in the city; but the greater number urged him to depart secretly. And so he did, to a little farm, not far from the city, and passed the time with a few companions, doing naught else but pray 20 night and day for all and for the Churches throughout the world, as was his custom. 2. And while praying he fell into a trance three days before he was taken, and saw his pillow being consumed by fire. And he turned and said to those with him, ' I must be burned alive.'

25 VI. 1. While his pursuers were still waiting for him, he went away to another farm, and immediately they followed close upon him. Not finding him, they laid hands on two young slaves, one of whom confessed under the torture. Now it was impossible Polycarp should escape, since his be- 30 trayers belonged to his own household. 2. And the justice of the peace whose lot it was to bear the same name as Herod, was in a hurry to bring him into the stadium, that he, being made partner with Christ, might fulfil his lot, and his betrayers might meet the same punishment as Judas.

35 VII. 1. Taking the young slave with them, the constables

and horsemen armed in the usual way went out on the
Preparation about the dinner-hour 'as against a thief' at a
run. Coming up in a body late in the day they found him
lying in a cottage in an upper room; he could indeed have
escaped from thence also elsewhere, but he refused, saying, 5
'The will of the Lord be done.' 2. Hearing then that
they were come he went down and talked with them, those
present marvelling at his great age and his constancy, and
at their excessive eagerness to take a man so old. So he
bade food and drink to be set before them at that hour, as 10
much as they wanted; and besought them to give him an
hour to pray undisturbed. 3. On leave being given he
stood and prayed, being so full of the grace of God that for
two hours he could not once be silent, and the hearers were
astonished, and many repented for having assailed an old 15
man so godlike.

VIII. 1. When at length he ended his prayer after
remembering all that ever had dealings with him, great and
small, well-known and unknown, and the whole Catholic
Church throughout the world, the time having now come for 20
his departure, they set him on an ass and brought him to the
city, it being a High Sabbath. 2. He was met by Herodes, the
High Sheriff, and by Herodes' father, Nicetes, who, having
transferred him to the carriage, sat down beside him, and
strove to persuade him with these words : 'What is the 25
harm of saying, "Caesar is Lord," and offering incense,'
with more to this effect, 'and saving your life'? At first he
made them no answer, but, when they persisted, he said :
'I do not intend to do as you advise me.' 3. Failing to
persuade him, they reviled him, and made him descend 30
with so much haste that in getting down from the carriage
he hurt his shin. He, as though nothing had happened,
paid no heed, but went on quickly with much eagerness on
his way to the stadium, where the din was so great that
none could be so much as heard.   35

IX. 1. As Polycarp entered the stadium, there came a
voice from heaven, saying, ' Be strong, Polycarp, and play
the man.' None saw the speaker, but the voice was heard
by those of our brethren who were present.   When he was
5 brought in, thereupon a great din arose as soon as they
heard ' Polycarp is taken '.

2. So the proconsul asked him whether he were the man.
And when he said ' Yes ', he tried to persuade him to deny
his faith, saying: ' Have respect to your age,' and other
10 such things as they were used to say: ' Swear by the
Fortune of Caesar, repent, say "Away with the Atheists".'
Polycarp, gazing with a steadfast countenance on all the
crowd of lawless heathen in the stadium, waved his hand
to them, sighed, and looking up to heaven said : ' Away
15 with the Atheists.'

3. When the proconsul pressed him further and said,
' Swear and I set you free : Curse Christ,' Polycarp
answered, ' Eighty and six years have I served Him, and
He did me no wrong. How can I blaspheme my King,
20 that saved me? '

X. 1. When the proconsul persevered saying: ' Swear
by the Fortune of Caesar,' Polycarp answered: ' If you
vainly imagine that I shall swear by the Fortune of Caesar,
as you say, and suppose that I know not what I am, hear
25 a plain answer, " I am a Christian." If you wish to learn
the Christian's reason, give me a day and listen.' 2. The
proconsul said : ' It is the people you must convince.'
Polycarp answered : ' I would have counted you worthy
to be reasoned with ; for we have been taught to give
30 honour as is fit, where we can without harm, to govern-
ments and powers ordained by God, but the people I do
not deem worthy to hear any defence from me.'

XI. 1. The proconsul said : ' I have beasts, and to them
I will throw you, unless you repent.' ' Bring them in,' he
35 answered, ' For repentance from the better to the worse

is no change to be desired, but it is good to change from cruelty to justice.'

2. The other spake again to him: ' If you despise the beasts, I will have you consumed by fire, unless you repent.' ' You threaten me,' answered Polycarp, ' with the fire that burns for an hour and is speedily quenched; for you know nothing of the fire of the judgement to come and of eternal punishment which is reserved for the wicked. Why delay? Bring what you will.'

XII. 1. While speaking these and many other words he grew full of confidence and joy, and his face was filled with grace, so that it fell out that not only was he not troubled by the things said to him, but on the contrary the proconsul was amazed and sent his own herald to proclaim thrice in the midst of the stadium, ' Polycarp has confessed himself to be a Christian.'

2. Upon this proclamation of the herald the whole multitude of heathen and Jews that dwelt in Smyrna cried aloud in ungovernable fury: ' This is the teacher of Asia, the father of the Christians, the destroyer of our Gods, who teaches many not to sacrifice or worship.' So saying they shouted beseeching Philip, the Asiarch, to let loose a lion on Polycarp. However, he said it was not lawful for him to do this, as he had concluded the wild beast combat. 3. Then they thought good to cry with one voice that Polycarp should be burnt alive. For it must needs be that the vision revealed to him on his pillow be fulfilled, when in prayer he saw it aflame, and turning to the faithful who were with him said in prophecy: ' I must be burned alive.'

XIII. 1. This then was brought about with great speed, more quickly than words can say, the crowd gathering together forthwith from the shops and baths wood and fuel, the Jews being particularly zealous in the work, as is their custom. 2. When the pyre was ready, he put off all his upper garments and undid his girdle, and endeavoured to take off his shoes, which he had not been used to do before because all the faithful used to contend with one another who should first touch his body. For even before his martyrdom he was treated with all honour for the goodness 5 of his life. 3. So he was immediately girded with the things devised for his burning; but when they were about to nail him to the stake as well, he said: ' Leave me as I am; for he that enabled me to abide the fire, will also enable me to abide at the stake unflinching without your safeguard 10 of nails.'

XIV. 1. So they bound him without nailing him. And he, with his hands bound behind him, like a choice ram taken from a great flock for sacrifice, an acceptable whole burnt-offering prepared for God, looked up to Heaven and 15 said: ' Lord God Almighty, Father of Thy well-beloved and blessed Son, Jesus Christ, through whom we have received the knowledge of Thee, God of Angels and Powers and of the whole creation and of all the race of the righteous who live before Thee, 2. I bless Thee that 20 Thou didst deem me worthy of this day and hour, that I should take a part among the number of the martyrs in the cup of Thy Christ to the resurrection of life eternal of soul and body in incorruption of the Holy Spirit: among whom may I be accepted before Thee to-day a rich and 25 acceptable sacrifice, as Thou didst fore-ordain and fore-show and fulfil, God faithful and true. 3. For this above all I praise Thee, I bless Thee, I glorify Thee through the Eternal and Heavenly High Priest Jesus Christ, Thy Well-beloved Son, through whom to Thee with Him and 30 the Holy Spirit be glory now and for evermore. Amen.'

XV. 1. When he had offered up the Amen, and finished his prayer, those who had charge of the fire set light to it. And a great flame blazing forth, we to whom it was given to behold, who were indeed preserved to tell the story to 35 the rest, beheld a marvel. 2. For the fire forming a sort of arch, like a ship's sail bellying with the wind, made a wall about the body of the martyr, which was in the midst, not like burning flesh, but like bread in the baking, or like gold and silver burning in a furnace. For we caught a most sweet perfume, like the breath of frankincense or some 5 other precious spice.

XVI. 1. At last when the impious people saw that his body could not be consumed by the fire they gave orders that a slaughterer should go and thrust a dagger into him. This being done there came forth [a dove and] such a gush 10 of blood that it put out the fire, and all the throng marvelled that there should be so great a difference between the unbelievers and the elect; 2. one of whom was the most admirable martyr, Polycarp, an apostolic and prophetic teacher of our time, and bishop of the Catholic 15 Church in Smyrna. For every word that he uttered from his mouth, was fulfilled then and shall be fulfilled hereafter.

XVII. 1. But the Adversary, that malicious and wicked one who is the enemy of the race of the just, seeing the 20 greatness of his witness, and the blamelessness of his life from the beginning, and that he was crowned with the crown of immortality, and had won a prize beyond gainsaying, made it his business that we might not even recover his body, though many were eager so to do and to touch 25 his sacred flesh. 2. At any rate he suggested to Nicetas, the father of Herodes and brother of Alce, to intreat the proconsul not to give us his body, ' Lest ', said he, ' They should abandon the Crucified, and begin to worship him.' The Jews made the same suggestions with much vehe- 30 mence, who also watched the body, when we were about to take it from the fire, not knowing that we can never abandon Christ who suffered for the salvation of those who are being saved throughout the whole world, the sinless for sinners, nor can we worship any other. 3. For Him, being 35 the Son of God, we adore, but the martyrs we love as disciples and imitators of the Lord, and rightly for their unsurpassable loyalty to their own King and Master; may it be granted us to have partnership and fellow-discipleship with them.

XVIII. 1. So the centurion, seeing the contentiousness of the Jews, set him in the midst and burnt him according to their custom. So we later took up his bones, being of more value than precious stones and more esteemed than gold, and laid them apart in a convenient place. 2. There the Lord will grant us to gather so far as may be and to celebrate with great gladness and joy the birthday of his martyrdom, in memory of those who have fought the good fight before us and for the training and preparation of those to come.

XIX. 1. Such is the story of the blessed Polycarp, who with the eleven from Philadelphia was martyred in Smyrna, and is more particularly remembered by all, so that he is spoken of in every place even by the Gentiles, having been not only a famous teacher, but also an illustrious martyr, whose martyrdom all desire to imitate, as being after the pattern of the gospel of Christ. 2. Having vanquished by his patience the unjust ruler, and thus received the crown of immortality he rejoices greatly with the apostles and with all the just, and glorifies the Almighty God and Father, and praises Our Lord Jesus Christ, the Saviour of our souls, the Pilot of our bodies, and the Shepherd of the Catholic Church throughout the world.

XX. 1. You indeed made request that the events might be described to you at greater length, but we for the present have declared them to you in brief by our brother Marcion. On receiving this send on the letter to the more distant brethren that they may glorify the Lord who makes choice of his own servants.

2. To Him that is able to bring us all by His grace and

bounty to His eternal kingdom through His Only-Begotten son Jesus Christ be glory, honour, power, and majesty for ever and ever. Salute all the Saints. Those with us, and Euarestus, the writer of this, with his whole house salute you. 5

XXI. The blessed Polycarp was martyred on the second day of the first part of the month Xanthicus, on the seventh day before the Kalends of March, on a High Sabbath, at the eighth hour. He was taken by Herodes, when Philip of Tralles was chief priest, in the proconsul- 10 ship of Statius Quadratus, in the everlasting reign of Jesus Christ; to whom be glory, honour, majesty, and a throne eternal, from generation to generation. Amen.

XXII. 1. We pray that you may be of good cheer, brethren, while you walk by the word of Jesus Christ 15 according to the Gospel: with whom be glory to God for the salvation of the elect Saints; even as Blessed Polycarp suffered martyrdom, in whose footsteps God grant that we may be found in the Kingdom of Jesus Christ.

2. This account was copied by Gaius from the papers of 20 Irenaeus, a disciple of Polycarp, Gaius having been himself a companion of Irenaeus. And I, Socrates, wrote it down in Corinth from the copy of Gaius. Grace be with you all.

3. I, Pionius, in my turn wrote it from the afore- 25 mentioned copy, having searched it out, for the blessed Polycarp made it known to me by revelation, as I shall show in what follows. I gathered it together when already almost worn away by time, that the Lord Jesus Christ may gather me also with His elect into His heavenly kingdom, 30 to Whom be glory with the Father and the Holy Spirit for ever and ever. Amen.

F

II

THE ACTS OF SS. CARPUS, PAPYLUS, AND AGATHONICA (A.D. 161-9)

THE martyrdom of these three martyrs is recorded by Eusebius, *Eccl. Hist.* iv. 15, 48, immediately after those of Polycarp and Pionius, all of which are referred to the same period—' of others who were martyred in Pergamus, a city of Asia, the records are still in circulation, i. e. of Carpus, Papylus, and a woman, Agathonica, who after many illustrious confessions were perfected with glory'. Harnack (*Texte*, iii. 3 f., pp. 440-54, 1888) gives the date as A.D. 161-9, the Emperors being M. Aurelius and L. Verus. Duchesne agrees (*Early Hist. of the Church*, Engl. trans., p. 194 note). J. de Guibert (*Revue des Questions historiques*, 83 (1908), pp. 5-23) puts the date later under Decius, whose persecution lasted from A.D. 250 to 251. Harnack says of these Acta : ' Their value is obvious.' Something has evidently been omitted in the account of S. Agathonica; she did not commit suicide, but was condemned, like the others, by the proconsul (v. p. 46, l. 6 note).   *Text from* KNOPF

1. WHILE the proconsul was in residence at Pergamus there were brought to him the blessed Carpus and Papylus, martyrs of Christ. 2. The proconsul having taken his seat on the tribunal said: ' What is your name? '

5 3. The blessed one answered: ' My first and chosen name is Christian, but, if you wish for my name in the world, Carpus.

4. The proconsul said: ' The commands of the Augusti are certainly known to you that you must both worship 10 the gods who govern the world; wherefore I counsel you both to come forward and sacrifice.'

5. Carpus said: ' I am a Christian, I worship Christ, the son of God, who came in the latter times for our salvation and delivered us from the deceit of the devil, and to such

idols I sacrifice not. 6. Do what you please, for it is impossible for me to sacrifice to counterfeit presentments of demons; for they who sacrifice to them are like them. 7. For as the " true worshippers "—those who, according to the divine teaching of our Lord, " worship God in spirit 5 and in truth "—are made like to the glory of God and are with Him immortal, partaking of the eternal life through the Word, so also those who serve these are made like to the vanity of the demons and perish with them in hell. 8. For they are justly punished along with him who 10 deceived man, the chosen creature of God, with him, I mean the Devil, who by his own wickedness provoked the demons thereto. Wherefore be assured, O proconsul, that I do not sacrifice to these.'

9. The proconsul said in anger: ' Sacrifice both of you 15 to the gods and do not play the fool.'

10. Carpus replied with a smile: ' Perish the gods that have not made the heaven and the earth ! '

11. The proconsul said: ' You must sacrifice: for so the Emperor commanded.' 20

12. Carpus answered: ' The living do not sacrifice to the dead.'

13. The proconsul said: ' Do the gods seem to you to be dead ? '

14. Carpus said: ' Would you hear the answer ? These 25 were never even men, nor ever lived, that they should die. 15. Do you wish to learn that this is true ? Take away from them your homage which you suppose they receive at your hands, and you shall know they are nothing, things of the earth earthy and destroyed by time. 16. For our 30 God who is timeless and made the ages Himself remains indestructible and everlasting, being ever the same and admitting neither of increase nor of decrease, but these are made by men and destroyed, as I said, by time. 17. And do not marvel that they give oracles and deceive. For the 35

Devil, having fallen in the beginning from his place of glory, would fain by his own villainy make of none effect the fatherly love of God for man, and being hard pressed by the Saints contends with them and prepares wars
5 beforehand and by forecast announces them to his own. 18. Likewise also from the things that happen to us daily he, being more ancient than the years, by his experience foretells the future evil which he himself intends to do. 19. For by the decree of God knowledge as well as wickedness
10 are his, and by God's permission he tempts man, seeking to turn him from holiness. 20. Be convinced therefore, O consular, that ye are living in no small folly.'

21. The proconsul said: ' By suffering much idle prate from you I have led you to blaspheme the gods and the
15 Augusti. So that it go no further with you, will you sacrifice? or what have you to say?'

22. Carpus answered: ' It is impossible for me to sacrifice, for I have never sacrificed to idols.'

23. So he at once ordered him to be hung up and
20 scraped. Carpus cried out: ' I am a Christian.' And after this torture had gone on for a long time, he was worn out and could speak no more.

24. So the proconsul, letting Carpus be, turned to Papylus, saying to him: ' Are you a councillor?'

25   25. And he answered: ' I am a citizen.'

26. The proconsul said: ' A citizen of what city?'

27. Papylus answered: ' Of Thyatira.'

28. The proconsul said: ' Have you any children?'

29. Papylus answered: ' Yes, and many of them, thanks
30 be to God!'

30. And one of the crowd shouted out saying: ' He means that some of the Christians are his children after his faith.'

31. The proconsul said: ' Why do you lie, saying that
35 you have children?'

32. Papylus answered: 'Would you learn that I do not lie, but speak the truth? In every district and city I have children in God.'

33. The proconsul said: 'Will you sacrifice? or what have you to say?'   5

34. Papylus answered: 'I have served God from my youth up, and I have never sacrificed to idols, but am a Christian, and you cannot hear more from me than this; for there is nothing greater or nobler than this for me to say.'   10

35. And he also was hung up and three times scraped with two instruments of torture at once, yet uttered no sound, but as a noble athlete withstood the wrath of the Enemy.

36. The proconsul seeing their exceeding patience ordered them to be burnt alive; and descending they both 15 hasted to the amphitheatre, that they might be rid quickly of the world. 37. Papylus was first to be nailed to the stake and lifted up, and on the fire's approach he prayed and gave up his soul in peace. 38. And Carpus being nailed after him smiled on them; and the bystanders were 20 astonished and said to him: 'What made you laugh?' 39. And the blessed said: 'I saw the glory of the Lord, and I was glad, and at the same time I was rid of you, and have no part in your misdeeds.' 40. When the soldier piled up the wood and lit it the sainted Carpus said as he hung: 'We 25 too were born of the same mother Eve and have the same flesh as you, but looking to the Judgement-seat of Truth let us endure all.' 41. When he had said this, on the fire's approach, he prayed saying: 'Blessed art Thou, Lord Jesus Christ, Son of God, because Thou didst deem me 30 also the sinner worthy of this part in Thee!' And having said this he gave up his soul.

42. A certain Agathonica standing and beholding the glory of the Lord, which Carpus said that he had seen, and perceiving the invitation to be from heaven, straight- 35

way lifted up her voice: 'This dinner hath been prepared
for me; of this glorious dinner therefore I must needs
partake and eat.'

43. But the people cried out, saying: 'Have pity on
your son.'

44. The blessed Agathonica said: 'He hath God Who
can have pity on him, for He is the Protector of all; but
I wherefore I am come' .... and having put off her outer
garments, she cast herself upon the stake rejoicing.   45
But those who saw it bewailed, saying: 'Terrible sentence, unjust orders!' 46. And being lifted up, when she
felt the fire touch her, she cried out thrice, saying: 'Lord,
Lord, Lord help me, for I flee unto Thee.'

47. And so she gave up the ghost, and was perfected
with the Saints, whose remains the Christians secretly took
up and carefully guarded to the glory of Christ and the
praise of His Martyrs, because to Him belong glory and
power, to the Father and to the Son and to the Holy
Spirit, now and always and for ever and ever.   Amen.

III

THE ACTS OF SS. JUSTIN AND HIS COMPANIONS
(A. D. 165)

S. JUSTIN was a Greek by birth, a native of Neapolis in Palestine, now Nablous, near the site of the Biblical Shechem. He went the round of several philosophies, applying first to a Stoic, who declared that a knowledge of God was unnecessary, then to a Peripatetic who was so greedy for fees that Justin doubted his being a philosopher at all, then to a Pythagorean, whose demand that he should first know music, astronomy, and geometry before beginning philosophy was too much for him, and finally to a Platonist, whose pupil he became. He had happened to be present at several martyrdoms, and been much moved. He then met a ' mysterious old man ' who ' led him from Plato to the Prophets, from metaphysics to faith in Christ ', and was converted about A. D. 133. Afterwards he came to Rome, and wrote a great deal on philosophical questions, and against heathen beliefs and Christian heresies. He still lived the philosophic life, wearing the characteristic short cloak, and acting in Eusebius's phrase (*Hist. Eccl.* iv. 11, 8) as ' an ambassador of the Divine word in the guise of a philosopher '. The only extant works of his which are certainly genuine are his two *Apologies*, of which the so-called ' Second ' is probably (v. Duchesne, *Early Hist. of the Chr. Ch.*, Engl. trans., p. 152) only an appendix to the first, addressed to the Emperor Antoninus Augustus (Pius), to the princes M. Aurelius and Lucius Verus, to the Senate, and to the Roman people, ' on behalf of those whom the whole human race hates and persecutes '; and the Dialogue with Trypho, in which he repeats, no doubt with amplifications, his dialogue with a Jew of that name twenty years before (*c.* A. D. 135) at Ephesus.

Just before his martyrdom in A. D. 165 he engaged in a public disputation with the Cynic, Crescens, and got the better of him. But Crescens, as Duchesne says, ' had other weapons at his command ', and worked, and with success, for his death. He was martyred in A. D. 165 with one woman, Charito, and five men, one of them, Euelpistus, a Cappadocian, a slave of the imperial house, another, Paeon, a bystander at the trial who volunteered his confession, 'a motley crew,' as Duchesne says, and pathetically characteristic of the universal appeal made by Christianity.

One of the most striking elements in his teaching is that the Divine Logos taught ' not only the Jewish Patriarchs, but those Greek philosophers who lived according to reason ' (Foakes Jackson, *Hist of the Chr. Ch.*, p. 159). His style is often crabbed and obscure (e.g. *Apol.* (1), ch. xv. 5 ; ch. xxiii. 3). It is, to my mind, one of the striking evidences of the authenticity of these Acts, that though too simple to be obscure, there is in Justin's answers a touch of precision, what one might call ' donnishness ', eminently characteristic of the philosopher. This note is found in such sentences as, ' To obey the commands of our Saviour Jesus Christ is not worthy of blame or condemnation ' (ch. ii.) ; (' what doctrines do you hold ?) ' I have endeavoured to make myself acquainted with all doctrines, but I have given my assent to the true doctrines of the Christians ' (*ib.*) ; ' yes, for the belief in accordance with which I follow them is right ' (*ib.*). Another point in which the Acts resemble the *Apology* is the insistence on the proof of the truth of Christianity from prophecy (Acts ii, *Apol.* (1), xxx foll.). And the noble and simple fortitude of Justin's answers in the fifth chapter of the Acts can be paralleled by passages in the *Apology*, such as that sentence which closes the second chapter : ' You can kill, but you cannot harm us.'

Text from KNOPF

I. IN the time of the wicked defenders of idolatry impious decrees were issued in town and country against the pious Christian folk to compel them to offer libations to vain idols. So the saints were seized and brought before
5 the prefect of Rome, by name Rusticus.

II. When they were brought before the judgement seat, Rusticus the prefect said to Justin : ' First of all obey the gods, and make submission to the Princes.'

Justin said : 'To obey the commands of our Saviour
10 Jesus Christ is not worthy of blame or condemnation.'

The prefect Rusticus said : ' What doctrines do you hold ? '

Justin said : ' I have endeavoured to make myself acquainted with all doctrines, but I have given my assent to the true doctrines of the Christians, whether they please the holders of false beliefs or no.'

The prefect Rusticus said : ' Do those doctrines please you, miserable man ? '

Justin said : ' Yes, for the belief in accordance with which I follow them is right.'

The prefect Rusticus said : ' What belief do you mean ? '

Justin said : ' That which we religiously profess concerning the God of the Christians, in whom we believe, one God, existing from the beginning, Maker and Artificer of the whole creation, seen and unseen; and concerning our Lord Jesus Christ, the Son of God, who hath also been proclaimed aforetime by the prophets as about to come to the race of men for herald of salvation and for master of true disciples. And I, being but a man, regard what I say to be of little worth in comparison of His Infinite God-head, but there is a power in prophecy, and that I acknowledge ; therein hath proclamation been made aforetime of Him of whom I just spoke as the Son of God. For I know that from the beginning the prophets foretold His coming among men.'

III. The prefect Rusticus said : ' Where do ye meet together ? '

Justin said : ' Where each wills and can. Do you really think that we all meet in the same place ? Not so: for the God of the Christians is not confined by place, but being unseen fills heaven and earth, and is worshipped and glorified by the faithful everywhere.'

The prefect Rusticus said: ' Tell me, where do ye meet, or in what place do you gather your disciples ? '

Justin said : ' I lodge above in the house of Martin,

near the baths of Timothy, and during all this time (this is my second visit to Rome) I have known no other place of meeting but his house. And if any wished to come to me, I imparted to him the word of truth.'

5 Rusticus said : ' To come to the point then, are you a Christian ? '

Justin said : ' Yes, I am a Christian.'

IV. The prefect Rusticus said to Chariton : 'Tell me further, Chariton, are you also a Christian ? '

10 Chariton said : ' I am a Christian by God's command'.

The prefect Rusticus said to Charito : 'What do you say, Charito ? '

Charito said : ' I am a Christian by God's gift.'

Rusticus said to Euelpistus : ' And what are you ? '

15 Euelpistus, a slave of Caesar, answered : 'I also am a Christian, freed by Christ, and share by the grace of Christ in the same hope.'

The prefect Rusticus said to Hierax : ' Are you also a Christian ? '

20 Hierax said : ' Yes, I am a Christian, for I worship and adore the same God.'

The prefect Rusticus said : ' Did Justin make you Christians ? '

Hierax said : ' I was, and shall ever be, a Christian ? '

25 A man called Paeon stood up and said : ' I also am a Christian.'

The prefect Rusticus said : ' Who taught you ? '

Paeon said : ' I received from my parents this good confession.'

30 Euelpistus said : ' I listened indeed gladly to the words of Justin, but I too received Christianity from my parents.'

The prefect Rusticus said : ' Where are your parents ? '

Euelpistus said : ' In Cappadocia.'

Rusticus said to Hierax : ' Where are your parents ? '

35 He answered, saying: ' Our true father is Christ, and our

mother our faith in Him. My earthly parents are dead, and I was dragged away from Iconium in Phrygia before coming hither.'

The prefect Rusticus said to Liberian : ' And what do you say? Are you a Christian? Are you an unbeliever 5 like the rest?'

Liberian said : ' I also am a Christian; for I am a believer and adore the only true God.'

V. The prefect said to Justin : ' Listen, you that are said to be a learned man, and think that you are acquainted 10 with true doctrine, if you shall be scourged and beheaded, are you persuaded that you will ascend to heaven?'

Justin said : ' I hope if I endure these things to have His gifts. For I know that for all who so live there abides until the consummation of the whole world the free gift of God.' 15

The prefect Rusticus said : ' Do you then think that you will ascend to heaven, to receive certain rewards?'

Justin said : ' I do not think, I know and am fully persuaded.'

The prefect Rusticus said : ' Let us now come to the 20 pressing matter in hand. Agree together and sacrifice with one accord to the gods.'

Justin said : ' No one who is rightly minded turns from true belief to false.'

The prefect Rusticus said : ' If ye do not obey, ye 25 shall be punished without mercy.'

Justin said : ' If we are punished for the sake of our Lord Jesus Christ we hope to be saved, for this shall be our salvation and confidence before the more terrible judge-ment-seat of our Lord and Saviour which shall judge the 30 whole world.' So also said the other martyrs : ' Do what you will. For we are Christians and offer no sacrifice to idols.'

Rusticus the prefect gave sentence : ' Let those who will not sacrifice to the gods and yield to the command 35

of the Emperor be scourged and led away to be beheaded
in accordance with the laws.'

VI. The holy martyrs went out glorifying God to the
customary place and were beheaded, and fulfilled their
5 testimony by the confession of their Saviour. And some
of the faithful took their bodies by stealth and laid them
in a convenient place, the grace of our Lord Jesus Christ
working with them, to whom be glory for ever and ever.
Amen.

IV

LETTER OF THE CHURCHES OF VIENNE AND LYONS

CONCERNING THE MARTYRDOM OF THE BISHOP S. POTHINUS AND MANY OTHERS (A. D. 177)

1. The Letter of the churches of Vienna and Lugdunum to the Churches of Asia and Phrygia is given by Eusebius in his *History of the Church*, Bk. V, chaps. 1 and 2, with a few omissions which he notes in their place. He introduces the letter thus : ' The most famous Churches in this region (the region in Gaul through which the Rhone flows) send the document dealing with the martyrs to the Churches in Asia and Phrygia, recording what happened to them in the following fashion : I will give it in their own words.'

2. Lugdunum (Lyons) and Vienna (Vienne) were situated, the first on the west, the second on the east bank of the Rhone, rather less than twenty miles apart. They were both important towns, Lugdunum the chief place in the province of Gallia Lugdunensis, Vienna in that of Gallia Narbonensis. It is interesting, in view of the harmony between the two Churches, that Tacitus notices the rivalry and enmity between the two towns.

3. Christianity, to judge from an inscription given by Le Blant (*Inscr. Chrét. de la Gaule*, vol. ii, no. 548), existed in Marseilles from the beginning of the second century. But this famous letter is the first important document of Gallic Christianity. What a hold it had already obtained there is shown by the fact that the successor of S. Pothinus, the Bishop of Lugdunum, whose martyrdom is here recorded, was S. Irenaeus, ' the most careful explorer of all kinds of learning,' as Tertullian calls him, the author of the famous book *Against Heresies*, written A. D. 180–5, only a few years after the martyrdoms described in his Epistle (A. D. 177). This is sufficient answer to those who have wished to post-date it, on the ground that it represents a Christianity too advanced for Gaul at that time. S. Irenaeus was a disciple of S. Polycarp (v. p. 31), himself a disciple of S. John, and

was the bearer of this letter. A dubious writer, possibly of the tenth century (Oecumenius, but his name and date are uncertain), describes him as its author, and his suggestion has been adopted by other scholars, but, if this had been the case, Eusebius would almost certainly have known and mentioned it.

The Christian Churches of Lugdunum and Vienna included Greeks of Asia, to whom the Bishop Pothinus, Irenaeus himself, Attalus one of the ' pillars ', Alexander, the doctor, Biblias, and Alcibiades (inf. p. 55 and note on p. 59, l. 16) belong. How strong this element was is shown by the direction of this letter. Others are Latins: Sanctus, Maturus, Blandina, Ponticus, Vettius Epagathus. In the list of 48 martyrs preserved in one of the Martyrologies there are 27 Latin, and 19 Greek names.

4. The date of the persecution was A. D. 177. The day of the martyrdom of SS. Blandina and her companions was August 1. Others died earlier, and they are all commemorated in the Martyrologies on June 2. The reigning Emperor was Marcus Aurelius Antoninus, the famous Stoic philosopher, who ruled from 161 to 180. It is a sad thing to find one of the greatest moralists of the world, the author of that noble book, *The Meditations*, among the persecutors. But there is no doubt of it: Lightfoot, *Apostolic Fathers*, pt. ii, vol. i, p. 526, says: ' The persecutions under M. Aurelius extend throughout his reign. They were fierce and deliberate. They were aggravated, at least in some cases, by cruel tortures. They had the emperor's direct personal sanction. They break out in all parts of the empire, in Rome, in Asia Minor, in Gaul, in Africa, possibly also in Byzantium.' The evidence comes from the Acts of Martyrs, from the Christian Apologists, from the heathen Celsus. SS. Justin and his companions, the Scillitan martyrs, SS. Cecilia, Carpus, Papylus, and Andronica, as well as others less famous, perished in this reign. It is true that M. Aurelius seems to have issued no edict against the Christians. The last legislation against them seems to have been the famous rescript of Trajan to Pliny, which forbade the Christians to be sought out officially, but commanded them to be tried when regularly accused, and, when obstinate, punished, but, if they recanted, dismissed. But the governors of provinces had very great powers, and often neglected imperial orders when they had lost their freshness.

This particular rescript of Trajan had to be re-enacted in the reigns both of Hadrian and of Antoninus Pius. M. Aurelius (§ 47) reminds the governor of one part of the rescript which he had neglected (§ 33), but discreetly passes over his violation of another. Avidius Cassius, a contemporary philosopher, says of this reign in particular that while M. Aurelius philosophized his governors did as they pleased. The truth is that the great moralist had (as Mason points out, *Hist. Mart.*, p. 33) ' a professional's contempt for a set of ignorant and self-taught amateurs', and a Stoic's dislike for the enthusiasm, almost levity, with which they faced death : ' This readiness for death must proceed from inward conviction, not come of mere perversity, like the Christians', but of a temper rational and grave, and, if it is to convince others, unostentatious ' (*Medit.* xi. 3, Rendall's trans.). M. Aurelius's aim was to be ' a man and a Roman ' (*ib.* ii. 5), he must therefore enforce the law against those who challenged authority, and refused the worship of Rome and the Augustus, but he would have done better to have remembered his own precept (*Medit.* viii. 59), ' Men exist for one another. Teach them then, or bear with them.'

5. There are two interesting passages which Eusebius appends to the Letter. The first, taken, so he tells us, from the Letter itself, illustrates the humility of the martyrs, and their dislike of any unnecessary, or self-assertive, asceticism—' One of them, Alcibiades, had lived a very hard life up till then, living on bread and water only, and attempted to do the same in prison. It was revealed to Attalus after the first contest which he accomplished in the amphitheatre, that Alcibiades was doing wrong in not using God's creatures, and was setting others an example that might be an offence to them. And Alcibiades yielded, and partook of all things freely, and gave thanks to God. For they were not unvisited by the grace of God, but the Holy Spirit was their counsellor ' (Eus. *Eccl. Hist.* v. 3).

The other is interesting from its reference to a famous heresy and for its mention of the great Irenaeus—' When Montanus and Alcibiades (not of course the Alcibiades above-mentioned but a Montanist leader) and Theodotus and their followers began then for the first time to be celebrated widely as prophets (for many miracles of Divine grace even then taking place in different Churches created a belief that they also were prophets); when a discussion arose about them, the brethren in Gaul subjoined to the same Letter their own judgement, a pious judgement in full accordance with the Faith (ὀρθοδοξοτάτην), on these matters also. They produced, moreover, different letters of the martyrs perfected amongst us, which, while still in prison, they had written to the brethren in Asia and Phrygia, nay even to Eleutherus the then Bishop of Rome, acting as ambassadors in the interest of the peace of the Churches. And these same martyrs commended also Irenaeus, at that time a priest of the diocese of Lyons, to the aforesaid bishop in Rome, bearing full testimony to him, as is expressed in their own words : " We pray for your welfare in all things and always in the Lord, father Eleutherus. We have charged our brother and colleague Irenaeus to convey this letter to you, and we beg you to regard him as commended to you, as one zealous for the covenant of Christ. For if we knew that rank gave any one a claim to righteousness, we would have begun by commending him as a priest of the Church, for so he is " ' (*Hist. Eccl.* v. 3 and 4).

The first part of this passage refers to the Montanists (for whom v. Introd. to *SS. Perp. and Fel.*, p. 76). Some have treated the Churches of Lyons and Vienne, and the martyrs in particular, as adherents of the Montanist heresy, which was rife in the province of Asia, especially in Phrygia. But there is no valid ground for this suspicion : ' Their judgement ' was, in Eusebius's opinion, ' pious and most orthodox ; ' their only object was, as men whose advice, on the brink of martyrdom, was highly valued, to do all they could to heal quarrels in the Church and promote peace.

Text from KNOPF

I. 3. THE servants of Christ dwelling in Vienne and Lyons to the brethren in Asia and Phrygia who have the same faith as we in redemption and the same hope, peace and grace and glory from God the Father and our Lord Christ
5 Jesus. 4. . . . The greatness of the tribulation here, and the exceeding wrath of the heathen against the Saints, and all that the blessed martyrs suffered, neither are we capable of describing accurately, nor can it be compassed in writing.

5. For the Adversary fell upon us with all his strength, making already a prelude to his coming in full force hereafter, and went to all lengths, practising and training his own against the servants of God, so that not only were we banished from houses and baths and market-places, but it was forbidden for any of us to be seen at all in any place whatsoever. 6. But the grace of God took the field against him, and protected the weak, and ranged on the other side steadfast pillars able through their endurance to draw on themselves all the onset of the Evil one; who also closed with him, bearing all kind of reproach and torment; who also, counting great things as small, made haste toward Christ, showing in very truth that ' the sufferings of this present time are not worthy to be compared with the glory that shall be revealed in us '.

7. And in the first place they endured nobly what the crowd in general heaped upon them, taunts, blows, halings, robberies, stone-throwings, beleaguerings, and all else that a furious multitude inflicts on private and public enemies. 8. And then they were brought into the market-place by the tribune of the soldiers and the magistrates of the city, and after being examined in the presence of the whole multitude and making their confession were shut up in prison until the arrival of the governor. 9. Afterwards they were brought before the governor, and he was showing all the usual cruelty towards us. Now among the brethren was Vettius Epagathus, one filled with the fullness of love towards God and his neighbour, whose conversation had been so rightly ordered that though young he did not fall below the witness borne to old Zacharias, he had indeed ' walked in all the commandments and ordinances of the Lord blameless ', and untiring in all service towards his neighbour, having great zeal for God and 'fervent in the spirit'. He being of this sort did not suffer the judgement so unreasonably being passed against us, but was indignant on our behalf, and claimed

to be heard himself, pleading in defence of the brethren that there was nothing godless or impious about us. 10. When those about the tribunal shouted him down (for he was a man of mark), and the governor did not allow
5 the just claim he put forward, but asked no more than this, whether he too were a Christian, he confessed in a loud voice and was added to the company of the martyrs. And he was styled the advocate of the Christians, having indeed the Advocate in himself, even the Spirit of Zacharias, which
10 he showed through the fullness of his love, being well pleased even to lay down his own life for the defence of the brethren. For he was and is a true disciple of Christ, ' following the Lamb whithersoever He goeth.'   .

11. After this the rest were divided: some were proto-
15 martyrs manifest and ready, who with all zeal fulfilled their confession even unto martyrdom; then too were manifested the unready, untrained, and still feeble, unable to bear the strain of a great contest. Of these about ten in number miscarried, who also wrought in us great sorrow
20 and grief immeasurable, and checked the zeal of those that had not yet been taken, but, in spite of all sorts of dreadful sufferings, nevertheless accompanied the martyrs and re-fused to leave them. 12. Then we were all greatly dis-traught from uncertainty about the confession, not from
25 fear of the torments that were coming upon us, but from looking to the end and dreading lest some should fall away. 13. There were taken however day by day those who were worthy, and these filled up their number, so that there were gathered from the two Churches all persons of merit
30 by whom more particularly affairs had been ordered here. 14. There were taken, too, certain pagan slaves of ours, since the governor had given public orders for all of us to be sought out. These by the lying in wait of Satan, in fear of the tortures which they saw the Saints suffering, and urged
35 thereto by the soldiers, falsely charged us with Thyestean

banquets and Oedipodean unions and with other crimes
which we are not permitted to mention or imagine, nor
even to believe that such things ever happened among men.

15. On the spread of these reports all were like wild
beasts against us, so that some who had formerly behaved 5
with moderation out of friendship were then greatly
enraged and gnashed their teeth at us. Then was fulfilled
what was spoken by our Lord that there should come a
time when ' whosoever killeth you will think that he doeth
God service '. 10

16. After this the holy martyrs endured tortures beyond
all telling, Satan being desirous that some blasphemous
word should escape their lips also. 17. Beyond measure all
the fury of crowd and governor and soldiers fell on Sanctus,
the deacon from Vienne, and on Maturus, newly baptized, 15
but a noble combatant, and on Attalus, a native of Pergamus, who had always been ' a pillar and stay ' of the
people here, and on Blandina, through whom Christ
made manifest that what things appear paltry and un-
comely and contemptible are accounted of great honour 20
with God, for their love to Him, which does not glory in
appearance but is shown in power.

18. For when we were all in fear, and her mistress
according to the flesh, herself a combatant among the
martyrs, was in agony lest Blandina should not be able 25
from weakness of body even to make her confession
boldly, she was filled with so much power that even those
who tortured her in relays in every way from morning
until evening were faint and weary. Indeed they themselves
confessed that they were beaten, having no longer any 30
more that they might do to her, wondering that she
remained alive, all her body being broken and torn, and
testifying that one kind of torture, let alone so many and
so grievous, was enough to release her soul. 19. But the
blessed woman, as a noble athlete, renewed her strength 35

in her confession, and it was refreshment and peace and freedom from pain amid her sufferings to repeat, ' I am a Christian, and there is no evil done among us.'

20. And Sanctus too endured nobly beyond all measure and all human patience all outrages at the hands of men, and, when the wicked hoped that because of the continuance and severity of the tortures something unseemly would be heard from him, with such constancy did he range himself against them that he uttered not his own name nor the name of the nation or city whence he came, nor whether he were bond or free; but to all questions answered in the Latin tongue, ' I am a Christian.' This he confessed repeatedly to serve for name and city and race and everything, and the heathen heard from him no other word.

21. Whence there arose great rivalry in the governor and the tormentors against him, so that when they had nothing more that they could do to him at the last they applied red-hot brazen plates to the most tender parts of his body. 22. And these indeed were burned, but he himself continued unbent and unyielding, stout in his confession, bedewed and strengthened by the heavenly fountain of the water of life issuing from the belly of the Christ. 23. His poor body was witness to his sufferings, for it was nothing but wound and weal, bent double, and robbed of the outward form of humanity, his body wherein Christ suffered and wrought great wonders, destroying the Adversary, and showing as a pattern to the rest that there is nothing terrible where is the love of the Father, nothing painful where the glory of Christ. 24. For when the wicked some days later tortured the martyr again and thought that his body being swollen and inflamed, if they applied the same torments they would overcome him, since he could not bear even a touch of the hand, or that by dying under torture he would frighten the rest, nothing of the sort happened in his case. Nay more, beyond all human

imagining his poor body revived and was restored in the later trial, and recovered its former appearance and the use of the limbs, so that the second torture became to him through the grace of Christ not a torment but a cure.

25. Moreover, there was a certain Biblias, one of those who had denied the faith, and the devil, who thought that he had already devoured her, wishing to damn her by blasphemy as well, brought her to torture, that he might force her to say impious things about us, being to start with frail and timid.

26. But she, while she was being tortured returned to her sober mind and woke as it were from a deep slumber, being reminded by her temporal punishment of the eternal torment in hell, and directly contradicted the blasphemers, saying: ' How can those eat children, who are forbidden to eat the blood even of brute beasts? ' And from this moment she confessed herself a Christian and was added to the company of the martyrs.

27. When the tyrants' cruelties were made of none effect by Christ through the patience of the martyrs, the devil set about contriving other devices, shutting them up in darkness in the foulest part of the prison, stretching their feet, strained to the fifth hole, in the stocks; with the other outrages which attendants angry, and full of the devil besides, are wont to inflict on prisoners ; so that most of them were suffocated in the prison, as many as the Lord, manifesting forth His glory, wished so to pass away. 28. For some after being so cruelly tormented, that it did not seem as if they could live any longer even if every attention were given them, lingered on in prison, destitute of all human care, but confirmed by the Lord, and strengthened in body and soul, encouraging and consoling the rest. Others, young and lately taken, whose bodies had not been already inured to torture, were unable to bear the burden of confinement and died there.

29. Blessed Pothinus, who had been entrusted with the charge of the bishopric in Lyons, being over ninety years of age and very sick in body, scarcely breathing from the sickness aforesaid, but strengthened by zeal of the spirit from his vehement desire for martyrdom, was dragged with the others on to the tribunal, his body fainting with old age and disease, but his soul sustained within him, that thereby Christ might triumph. 30. He was conveyed by the soldiers on to the tribunal, accompanied by the magistrates of the city and the whole multitude who cried this and that ; accusing him of being also one of Christ's followers, and he ' witnessed a good confession '. 31. Being questioned by the governor who was the God of the Christians, he answered: ' If you are worthy, you shall know.' After this he was hustled without mercy, and suffered hurts of all kinds : for those who were close showed him all manner of insolence with hand and foot, not reverencing his years, and those at a distance hurled at him anything each might have ready, all deeming that any one was guilty of great offence and impiety, who was behindhand in brutality towards him; for they thought in this way to avenge their gods. So he was cast scarcely breathing into the prison, and after two days expired.

32. And here took place a great dispensation of God, and there was manifested the immeasurable mercy of Christ, after a fashion rarely known among the brotherhood, but worthy of Christ's devising. 33. For those who when first taken denied the faith were imprisoned like the rest and shared their sufferings; for their denial was of no profit to them at all at that time, since those who confessed to be what indeed they were were imprisoned as Christians, having no other charge brought against them, while the others were detained as murderers and villains, being punished twice as hardly as the rest. 34. For those were comforted by the joy of their martyrdom, and the

hope of the promises, and by love towards Christ, and the Spirit of the Father, whereas these were greatly tormented by their conscience, so that as they passed they were easily distinguished by their looks from all the rest. 35. For those advanced full of joy, having in their looks a mingling of majesty and great beauty, so that even their chains were worn by them as a comely ornament, as for a bride adorned with fringed raiment of gold richly wrought, exhaling at the same time the ' sweet savour of Christ ', so that some thought they had been anointed with perfume of this world, but these downcast, dejected, ill-favoured, full of all unseemliness, taunted beside by the heathen as base and cowardly, bearing the reproach of murderers, but having lost their universally honourable and glorious and life-giving name. The rest seeing this were strengthened, and those who were taken afterwards made their confession undoubtingly, giving not so much as a thought to the devil's arguments.

36. [After some further remarks they continue.] After this their martyrdoms were parcelled into deaths of all sorts. For plaiting one crown of different colours and all kinds of flowers they offered it to the Father; it was needful indeed that the noble athletes should endure a manifold conflict and win a great victory before they received the great crown of immortality.

37. Maturus, then, and Sanctus and Blandina and Attalus were taken into the amphitheatre to the beasts to give the heathen a public spectacle of cruelty, a special day being appointed because of our brothers for a fight with beasts. 38. And Maturus and Sanctus again went in the amphitheatre through every form of torture, as though they had suffered nothing at all before; or rather, as having overcome the adversary already in many bouts, and contending now for the final crown of victory, they bore the usual running of the gauntlet of whips, and the mauling

by the beasts, and everything else that the maddened people, on this side or on that, clamoured for and demanded, and on the top of all the iron chair, whereon their bodies were roasted and filled with the savour the nostrils of the 5 people. 39. But they did not rest even so, but were more mad than ever, in their desire to overcome the martyrs' endurance, yet not even then did they hear from Sanctus aught else save the word of his confession he had been wont to utter from the beginning. 40. These, then, after 10 their spirits had long held out through a great contest, when in place of all the diversity of single combats they had been throughout that day a spectacle to the world, were offered up at last. 41. But Blandina was exposed hung on a stake to be the food of the beasts let loose on her. Alike by the 15 sight of her hanging in the form of a cross and by her earnest prayer she put much heart in the combatants; for they saw during the contest even with the eyes of flesh in the person of their sister Him who was crucified for them, to assure those who believed on Him that every one who 20 suffereth for the glory of Christ hath for ever fellowship with the living God. 42. And as none of the beasts at that time touched her, she was taken down from the stake and brought back again to the prison, to await another contest, that having won in many trials she might make that 25 ' crooked Serpent's ' condemnation irreversible, and inspire her brethren—she, the little, the weak, the contemptible— who had put on Christ, the great and invincible athlete, and had worsted in many bouts the adversary, and through conflict crowned herself with the crown of immortality. 30   43. Attalus, too, being loudly called for by the crowd (for he was a man of repute), entered the arena as a combatant well-prepared by his good conscience, for he was soundly trained in the Christian discipline, and had ever been a witness to truth amongst us. 44. He was being led 35 round the amphitheatre with a placard preceding him, on

which was written in Latin: ' This is Attalus the Christian,' the people being violently inflamed against him,
when the governor learning that he was a Roman citizen
ordered him to be remanded with the rest that were in the
prison, and, having written a dispatch to Caesar concerning 5
them, waited his sentence.

45. The interval was not idle nor unfruitful to them,
but through their patience was made manifest the immeasurable mercy of Christ. For the dead were made
alive through the living, and martyrs showed kindness to 10
those who were not martyrs, and there was much joy in
the heart of the Virgin Mother, in recovering alive those
untimely births she had cast forth as dead. 46. For through
them the most part of those who had denied the faith
entered again into their mother's womb, and were con- 15
ceived again, and quickened again, and learned to make
their confession, and alive already and braced came to the
tribunal (for He who hath no pleasure in the death of the
wicked made sweet their bitterness, and God was gracious
to them unto repentance), that they might again be ques- 20
tioned by the governor. 47. For the command of Caesar
was that these should be beheaded, but that those who
denied the faith should be set free. So as it was the
beginning of the festival here (it is thronged by an assem-
blage of all peoples), the governor brought the blessed ones 25
to the tribunal, making a gazing-stock and a show of them
to the multitude. Therefore he examined them again,
and beheaded those who appeared to possess Roman citizen-
ship, and sent the rest to the beasts.

48. And Christ was greatly glorified in those who had 30
formerly denied the faith, but then contrary to the expectation of the heathen made their confession. For they were
privately examined with the intent they should be set free,
and confessing were added to the company of the martyrs.
There remained outside those who had never had even 35

a vestige of the faith, nor any knowledge of the wedding
garment, nor any thought of the fear of God, but through
their conversation blasphemed the Way, that is the sons
of perdition.

5   49. All the rest were added to the Church. As they
were being examined, a certain Alexander, Phrygian by
birth, doctor by profession, who had spent many years in
the Gauls, and was known to almost all for his love to
God and his boldness in preaching the Word (for he was
10 not without a share in the Apostolic gift), was standing
by the tribunal and urging them by signs to confession,
and so became manifest to those surrounding the tribunal
as one in travail. 50. The multitude, angered at the renewed confession of those who had formerly denied the
15 faith, clamoured against Alexander as the cause of this.
So when the governor had ordered him to be set before
him, and asked him who he was, Alexander said: ' A
Christian.' The governor in anger condemned him to
the beasts, and on the next day he entered the arena with
20 Attalus. For to gratify the people the governor had given
Attalus also to the beasts, for the second time. 51. And
when they had gone through all the instruments devised
for torture in the amphitheatre, and had endured a contest
very great, they also were offered up at last. Alexander,
25 indeed, neither groaned nor uttered any sound at all, but
communed in his heart with God. 52. But Attalus, when
he had been placed in the iron chair, and was burning
everywhere, as the savour from his body was rising upward, said to the multitude in the Latin tongue: ' Lo!
30 as for eating of men, this is what you yourselves do ; but
we neither eat men nor work any other wickedness.' And
being asked what was the name of God, he answered:
' God hath no name as man hath.'

      53. After all these, on the last day of the single combats,
35 Blandina was again brought in with Ponticus, a boy of

about fifteen. They had also been led in daily to look upon
the torture of the rest, and their enemies would fain have
forced them to swear by their idols; but because they continued steadfast and made nought of them, the multitude
was enraged against them, so that they neither pitied the 5
age of the boy, nor reverenced the sex of the woman. 54.
They exposed them to every terror, they made them pass
through every torment in turn, again and again constrain-
ing them to swear, but unable to achieve their purpose.
For Ponticus, encouraged by his sister, so that even the 10
heathen saw that she was exhorting and strengthening him,
after nobly enduring every torment gave up the ghost.

55. The blessed Blandina last of all, like a noble mother
that has encouraged her children and sent them before
her crowned with victory to the King, retracing herself 15
also all her children's battles hastened towards them,
rejoicing and triumphing in her departure, as though she
were called to a marriage supper, instead of being cast to
the beasts. 56. After the whips, after the beasts, after the
frying-pan, she was thrown at last into a net, and cast 20
before a bull. And after being tossed for some long time
by the beast, having no further sense of what was happen-
ing because of her hope and hold on the things she had
believed, and because of her communing with Christ, she was
herself also offered up, the very heathen confessing that 25
they had never known a woman endure so many and so
great sufferings.

57. But not even so were their madness and savagery
towards the Saints appeased. For wild and barbarous
peoples stirred up by that wild Beast were hard to satisfy, 30
and their cruelty found another and peculiar outlet upon
the bodies of the dead. 58. For because they lacked human
reason their defeat did not shame them, rather it fired their
beast-like fury, both governor and people showing towards
us the same undeserved hatred, that the Scripture might be 35

fulfilled: ' He that is wicked, let him do wickedly still, and he that is righteous let him do righteousness still.' 59. For those that were suffocated in the prison they threw to the dogs, watching carefully by night and day, lest we 5 should give any of them burial. After that they exposed what the beasts and the fire had left, part torn, part charred, and the heads of the rest with the trunks; these likewise they left unburied, and watched them for many days with a guard of soldiers. 60. Some raged and gnashed their 10 teeth at the dead, seeking to take some more exquisite revenge upon them. Others laughed and mocked, magnifying at the same time their idols, and attributing to them the punishment of the martyrs. Others again who were more reasonable and seemed to have some degree of feeling 15 for us reproached us, repeating: ' Where is their God, and how did their religion which they preferred even to their lives profit them? ' 61. On their side such were the varieties of behaviour; on ours there was great sorrow because we could not bestow the bodies in the earth. For 20 night did not help us towards this, nor money persuade, nor prayer shame, but they watched every way, as though they would derive some great profit from the martyrs' loss of burial. [Then after some further remarks they go on.] 62. So the bodies of the martyrs, after being subjected to 25 all kinds of contumely and exposed for six days, were then burnt and reduced to ashes by the impious, and swept into the river Rhone which flows hard by, that not a fragment of them might be left on earth. 63. And they planned this, as though they could get the better of God, and rob 30 them of the other Life; that, in their own words, ' They may have no hope of resurrection, trusting in which they introduce among us a strange and new religion, and despise tortures, going readily and with joy to death. Let us see now whether they will rise again, and whether their God 35 can help them and deliver them from our hands.'

II. [1. Such are the things that happened to the churches of Christ in the time of the aforesaid Emperor, from which one may reasonably conjecture what took place in the other provinces. It is worth while adding thereto other passages from the same document, in which the gentleness 5 and kindness of the aforesaid martyrs have been described in the exact words that follow.]

2. So completely did they emulate and imitate Christ, who ' being in the form of God thought it not a prize to be on an equality with God ', that, though they had 10 reached such a height of glory and had borne witness not once nor twice but often, and had been brought back alive from the beasts bearing about them burns and weals and wounds, they neither proclaimed themselves to be martyrs, nor suffered us to address them by that name, but, 15 if ever any one of us by letter or by word of mouth called them martyrs, they rebuked him sharply. 3. For they gladly yielded the title of Martyr to Christ, the faithful and true witness and first-begotten of the dead and Prince of the Life of God, and they remembered the martyrs already 20 departed, and said: ' They are already martyrs, whom Christ thought worthy to be taken up in the hour of their confession, having sealed their witness by their death, but we are ordinary humble confessors.' And with tears they exhorted the brethren, beseeching them that earnest 25 prayer might be offered for them to be made perfect.

4. And, though they showed the power of martyrdom in deed, speaking with much boldness to all the heathen, and made manifest their nobleness by their patience and fearlessness and fortitude, yet they begged not to be given the 30 title of Martyr among the brethren, being filled with the fear of God.

5. [And a little later they say.] They humbled themselves under the mighty hand, by which they have now been greatly exalted. Then, however, they gave a reason 35

for their faith to all, but accused none; they loosed all, but bound none; and prayed for those who cruelly used them, as did Stephen, the perfect martyr: ' Lord, lay not this sin to their charge.' And if he prayed for those who stoned
5 him, how much more for the brethren.

6. [And again later.] This on account of the sincerity of their love was the greatest of all their contests with the Devil, that the Beast being throttled might disgorge alive those whom he at first thought to have devoured. For
10 they did not boast themselves against the fallen, but wherein they themselves abounded gave to those that lacked, having a mother's tender mercy, and shedding many tears on their behalf unto the Father.

7. They asked for life, and He gave it them, which they
15 shared with their neighbours, and departed to God all ways victorious. Having loved peace ever, and ever commended peace to us, they went in peace to God, leaving no sorrow to their Mother, nor strife and war to their brethren, but joy and peace and concord and love.

20 [8. Let these things concerning the love of those blessed ones for their brethren who had fallen away be profitably set forth because of the inhuman and pitiless behaviour of those who thereafter bore themselves mercilessly toward the members of Christ.]

V

THE ACTS OF THE SCILLITAN SAINTS

(JULY 17, A.D. 180)

SCILLIUM was a see in Africa Proconsularis, suffragan of Carthage. The Acts of Martyrdom of the Christians condemned
to death by the sword in that place are the most ancient Acts in
existence for the Roman Province of Africa. They, like the
Acts of S. Cyprian, are among the best examples of that class
of Acts which is founded on official reports, but are even more
perfect than those, in the sense that there is even less added by
the editor. There are numerous versions, that from which the
text is taken is from a manuscript in the British Museum discovered by the Dean of Wells (*Texts and Studies*, I. ii, pp. 112–
16). This discovery not only cleared up several difficulties,
especially about the date of the Martyrdom, but gave us a text
of singular conciseness, and simplicity and of a severe and
unadorned beauty. *Text from* ARMITAGE ROBINSON.

IN the consulship of Praesens, then consul for the second
time, and Claudian, on the 17th of July, Speratus,
Nartzalus and Cittinus, Donata, Secunda, Vestia were
brought to trial at Carthage in the council-chamber. The
proconsul Saturninus said to them: 'You may merit 5
the indulgence of our Lord the Emperor, if you return to
a right mind.'

Speratus said: 'We have never done harm to any, we
have never lent ourselves to wickedness; we have never
spoken ill of any, but have given thanks when ill-treated, 10
because we hold our own Emperor in honour.'

The proconsul Saturninus said: 'We also are religious
people, and our religion is simple, and we swear by the
genius of our Lord the Emperor, and pray for his safety,
as you also ought to do.' 15

Speratus said: 'If you will give me a quiet hearing,
I will tell you the mystery of simplicity.'

Saturninus said: 'If you begin to speak evil of our sacred rites, I will give you no hearing; but swear rather by the genius of our Lord the Emperor.'

Speratus said: 'I do not recognize the empire of this 5 world; but rather I serve that God, whom no man has seen nor can see. I have not stolen, but if I buy anything, I pay the tax, because I recognize my Lord, the King of kings and Emperor of all peoples.'

The proconsul Saturninus said to the rest: 'Cease to 10 be of this persuasion.'

Speratus said: 'The persuasion that we should do murder, or bear false witness, that is evil.'

The proconsul Saturninus said: 'Have no part in this madness.'

15 Cittinus said: 'We have none other to fear save the Lord our God who is in heaven.'

Donata said: 'Give honour to Caesar as unto Caesar, but fear to God.'

Vestia said: 'I am a Christian.'

20 Secunda said: 'I wish to be none other than what I am.'

The proconsul Saturninus said to Speratus: 'Do you persist in remaining a Christian?'

Speratus said: 'I am a Christian.' And all consented 25 thereto.

The proconsul Saturninus said: 'Do you desire any space for consideration?'

Speratus said: 'When the right is so clear, there is nothing to consider.'

30 The proconsul Saturninus said: 'What have you in your case?'

Speratus said: 'The Books, and the letters of a just man, one Paul.'

The proconsul Saturninus said: 'Take a reprieve of 35 thirty days and think it over.'

Speratus again said: ' I am a Christian.' And all were
of one mind with him.

The proconsul Saturninus read out the sentence from
his note-book: ' Whereas Speratus, Nartzalus, Cittinus,
Donata, Vestia, Secunda, and the rest have confessed 5
that they live in accordance with the religious rites of
the Christians, and, when an opportunity was given them
of returning to the usage of the Romans, persevered in
their obstinacy, it is our pleasure that they should suffer
by the sword.'   10

Speratus said: ' Thanks be to God! '

Nartzalus said: ' To-day we are martyrs in heaven:
thanks be to God! '

The proconsul Saturninus commanded that proclamation be made by the herald: ' I have commanded that 15
Speratus, Nartzalus, Cittinus, Veturius, Felix, Aquilinus,
Laetantius, Januaria, Generosa, Vestia, Donata, Secunda
be led forth to execution.'

They all said: ' Thanks be to God! '

And so all were crowned with martyrdom together, and 20
reign with the Father and Son and Holy Spirit for ever
and ever. Amen.

VI

THE PASSION OF SS. PERPETUA AND FELICITAS

(MARCH 7, A. D. 203)

THE martyrdom of SS. Perpetua and Felicitas and their companions holds a place of its own among the early martyrdoms. Apart from its peculiar beauty it has three special points of interest :

1. Chapters iii–x claim to have been written by Perpetua herself, chaps. xi–xiii by Saturus, another of the martyrs. No one who has any sense of style can doubt that the author of the remainder of the Acts is a different person from the writers of these chapters. His work is that of a man accustomed to composition, his sentences are often of considerable length and periodic in structure, he is fond of epigram, he is often difficult (v. inf.). Their writing, on the other hand, is marked by extreme simplicity and a complete absence of literary artifice. Thus, as the Dean of Wells has pointed out, the sentences both of Perpetua and Saturus are usually connected by ' et ' (' and '), Perpetua employs it 152 times in 172 lines, Saturus 57 times in 52 lines, the editor, as he may be called, only 90 times in 170 lines. That is to say, Perpetua and Saturus lay their thoughts simply side by side, the editor subordinates his one to another to show their logical connexion. Again Perpetua repeats words, where a practised writer, like the editor, varies them. Chapter vi will illustrate both of these points, notice the number of ' ands ', and the repetition of the words ' and I answered ', ' grieve; ' also the Latin word for ' overthrow my resolution ' and ' thrown down ' is the same. So in ch. iii ' few days ', ' anxiety ', ' anxious', ' prison ', ' baby ' recur repeatedly. She is also fond of certain words, she alone uses ' deicere ' in the sense of ' overthrowing a person's resolution ', and she uses it three times (chaps. iii, v, vi), ' refrigerare ' ' to refresh one self ' comes four times in Perpetua (chaps. iii, viii, ix), once in Saturus (xiii), never in the editor except when he is quoting Perpetua, or referring to her use of the word (xvi twice). A still more interesting fact is that Perpetua, who, as Saturus tells us (ch. xiii), could speak Greek,

uses ten transliterated Greek words, Saturus four, and the editor five (two of them in quoting or referring to words of Perpetua), and all those used by the two last are ' familiar Bible or Church phrases ', whereas among those used by Perpetua are several uncommon religious words, and some quite unconnected with religion. We have very little of Saturus's writing, but there is some individuality in that little, e. g. he uses ' viridarium ', where Perpetua uses ' hortus ', for a ' garden '. But his two most striking peculiarities are (a) his use of the words ' I said ', ' he said ', ' they said ' without variation, and (b) a love for vague, indeterminate phrases, e.g. ' like as it might be ' (' talis quasi ') in chaps. xi and xii, and the use of ' ceteri ' ' the other ' five times in the same chapters. These two peculiarities are suggestive of an education inferior to that of Perpetua. We all know how fond uneducated people are of phrases like ' in a manner of speaking ', ' a sort of ', ' as you might say ', and no one who has read young boys' essays can have failed to notice their love of vagueness, due to want of vocabulary or want of precision in thought ; and the recurrence of ' says he ', ' says I ' is an equally familiar trait. The general result of the examination is that we may thoroughly trust the attribution of these chapters to Perpetua and Saturus respectively.

2. The second point of interest is the authorship of the other chapters. As early as the middle of the seventeenth century it was suspected that the great Tertullian, the contemporary of Perpetua and the greatest African writer of the time, was their author. The chief reasons for this belief are these :

A. In these chapters we do not find mere description with pious comment, but, especially in the Preface, reasoned statements of the significance of martyrdom, and the value of visions. The author speaks with authority, as one whose words have weight.

B. There is a strong resemblance between Tertullian's treatment of martyrdom and that of the author of these chapters. Both speak of the ' glory of God ' as the great end of martyrdoms (v. ch. i, note). Both write of martyrdom as a Second Baptism, it is indeed a commonplace with Tertullian (v. chs. xviii, xxi). Both dwell on the work of the Holy Spirit in this connexion, compare chaps. i, xx, and the conclusion in ch. xxi with Tert., *de Cor.* i, ' It remains for those who have rejected the prophecies of the same Spirit to think about refusing martyrdom also ', and *ad Mart.* i, ' First of all therefore, ye blessed ones, do not sadden the Holy Spirit who has entered the prison with you. For if He had not entered with you now, you would not have been there to-day '. Compare also with these chapters the *de Patientia* of Tertullian throughout, the picture of Patience there seems drawn from that of Perpetua here. There is much likeness between them in word and phrase and syntax. One example of this is given in the note on p. 78, l. 12. The Dean of Wells gives many others. Moreover, a very striking coincidence, in two quotations, that from Acts, ii. 17 and that from 1 John i. 1–3 (both in ch. i) the same divergences from the text as we have it occur in our author and in Tertullian (*adv. Marc.* v. 8, and *adv. Prax.* xv).

C. The history of the text is remarkable. There is only one complete Latin text (Cod. Casinensis). The Greek translation has modified passages in chaps. i and xvi (v. Robinson), and has spoilt the conclusion. The two other Latin texts (Cod. Salisbury and Cod. Compend.), and the short Latin version, which was made for use in the Church services, have omitted the whole of the Preface (ch. i). There was clearly some prejudice against the work of the editor. To what was this due ?

There was at the time of Perpetua's martyrdom a heretical sect, known as Montanists from its founder Montanus, which believed in the direct inspiration of men and women, women especially, by the Holy Spirit, who spoke through them by visions and prophecies and ecstatic utterances of all kinds, in the duty of rigorous asceticism, and in an immediate Second Coming. It gave women a high place in the Church, even admitting them, it is said, to the presbyterate and episcopate. Tertullian became a Montanist about A. D. 205. Now in these Acts, and particularly in the work of the editor, there is a strong, but quite orthodox, insistence on the work of the Spirit, and on the importance of visions, i. e. on doctrines which the Montanists exaggerated to the point of heterodoxy. The suspicion, shown in the successive textual alterations, of the work of the editor is, I contend, an indirect proof that he was Tertullian. It is noticeable that the prejudice is confined to the work of the editor, and does not extend to the Visions.

Why then was Tertullian's name never mentioned ? There are two possible reasons for the silence. Some may have known that the author of these chapters was suspect without knowing his name ; others who knew it would be unwilling to mention it for fear of casting a slur on these famous Acts, which were deeply reverenced, and read aloud in church (Augustine, *Serm.* 280, ch. i, and 282, ch. ii).

3. The third point of interest is the Visions of SS. Perpetua and Saturus. S. Augustine refers to them repeatedly, *de Anima,* i. 10 ; iii. 9, where his warning against their being put on a level with canonical Scriptures shows the general reverence for them ; cf. also *Serm.* 280, 281. An anonymous homily on Polyeuctus (suffered *c.* A. D. 250), delivered a little after A. D. 363 (Aubé, *Polyeucte dans l'histoire,* p. 77) refers to the vision of the 'heavenly stairs' (ch. iv).

The Divine vision is distinguished from the Satanic or hallucinatory by its effects, persistent light, Divine love, peace of soul, inclination towards the things of God, the constant fruits of sanctity (cf. Ignatius, *Spir. Exercises,* 'Rules for the discernment of Spirits '). Judged by these criteria the visions of Perpetua and Saturus are clearly marked as Divine, for they encouraged and guided both martyrs (v. chaps. x and xii). One thing more about these visions. They are none the less to be regarded as sent by God, that there is in them reminiscences of earthly experiences, especially of the services of the Church. An 'imaginative ' vision, in which there is a ' sensible representation of objects by the action of the imagination alone ', however Divine, must communicate itself through forms and images which can be understood, it will not be a mere transcript of the subject's earthly experience, but it must contain incidents from it, and Tertullian himself (*de Anima,* 9), speaking of a woman who had revelations, says that the material for her visions was supplied from the scriptures read, the psalms sung, and the prayers offered in the Church services. I have tried to indicate the sources of such incidents in the notes.

The scene of the martyrdom was the amphitheatre at Carthage.

Text from ARMITAGE ROBINSON (*and* KNOPF)

(*From the Latin*)

I. IF the ancient examples of faith, such as both testified to the grace of God, and wrought the edification of man, have for this cause been set out in writing that the reading of them may revive the past, and so both God be glorified
5 and man strengthened, why should not new examples be set out equally suitable to both those ends? For these in like manner will some day be old and needful for posterity, though in their own time because of the veneration secured to antiquity they are held in less esteem. But let them see
10 to this who determine the one power of the one Spirit by times and seasons: since the more recent things should rather be deemed the greater, as being ' later than the last '. This follows from the pre-eminence of grace promised at the last lap of the world's race. For ' In the last days,
15 saith the Lord, I will pour forth of My Spirit upon all flesh, and their sons and their daughters shall prophesy: and on my servants and on my handmaidens will I pour forth of My Spirit: and their young men shall see visions, and their old men shall dream dreams '. And so we who
20 recognize and hold in honour not new prophecies only but new visions as alike promised, and count all the rest of the powers of the Holy Spirit as intended for the equipment of the Church, to which the same Spirit was sent bestowing all gifts upon all as the Lord dealt to each man, we cannot
25 but set these out and make them famous by recital to the glory of God. So shall no weak or despairing faith suppose that supernatural grace, in excellency of martyrdoms or revelations, was found among the ancients only; for God ever works what He has promised, to unbelievers a wit-
30 ness, to believers a blessing. And so ' what we have heard and handled declare we unto you also ', brothers and little children, ' that ye also ' who were their eyewitnesses may be reminded of the glory of the Lord, and you who now learn

by the ear ' may have fellowship with ' the holy martyrs,
and through them with the Lord Jesus Christ, to whom
belong splendour and honour for ever and ever. Amen.

II. Certain young catechumens were arrested, Revocatus and his fellow-slave Felicitas, Saturninus, and
Secundulus. Among these also Vibia Perpetua, well-born,
liberally educated, honourably married, having father and
mother, and two brothers, one like herself a catechumen,
and an infant son at the breast. She was about twenty-two
years of age. The whole story of her martyrdom is from
this point onwards told by herself, as she left it written,
hand and conception being alike her own.

III. " When I was still, she says, with my companions,
and my father in his affection for me was endeavouring to
upset me by arguments and overthrow my resolution,
' Father,' I said, ' Do you see this vessel for instance lying
here, waterpot or whatever it may be? ' ' I see it,' he said.
And I said to him, ' Can it be called by any other name
than what it is? ' And he answered, ' No.' ' So also I
cannot call myself anything else than what I am, a
Christian.'

Then my father, furious at the word ' Christian ', threw
himself upon me as though to pluck out my eyes; but he
was satisfied with annoying me; he was in fact vanquished,
he and his devil's arguments. Then I thanked the Lord for
being parted for a few days from my father, and was
refreshed by his absence. During those few days we were
baptized, and the Holy Spirit bade me make no other
petition after the holy water save for bodily endurance.
A few days after we were lodged in prison; and I was in
great fear, because I had never known such darkness.
What a day of horror! Terrible heat, thanks to the
crowds! Rough handling by the soldiers! To crown all
I was tormented there by anxiety for my baby. Then
Tertius and Pomponius, those blessed deacons who were

ministering to us, paid for us to be removed for a few hours
to a better part of the prison and refresh ourselves. Then
all went out of the prison and were left to themselves.
[My baby was brought to me], and I suckled him, for he
5 was already faint for want of food. I spoke anxiously to
my mother on his behalf, and strengthened my brother,
and commended my son to their charge. I was pining
because I saw them pine on my account. Such anxieties
I suffered for many days; and I obtained leave for my baby
10 to remain in the prison with me; and I at once recovered
my health, and was relieved of my trouble and anxiety
for my baby; and my prison suddenly became a palace to
me, and I would rather have been there than anywhere
else.

15　　IV. Then my brother said to me: ' Lady sister, you are
now in great honour, so great indeed that you may well
pray for a vision and may well be shown whether suffering
or release be in store for you.' And I who knew myself
to have speech of the Lord, for whose sake I had gone
20 through so much, gave confident promise in return,
saying: 'To-morrow I will bring you word.' And I made
request, and this was shown me. I saw a brazen ladder of
wondrous length reaching up to heaven, but so narrow
that only one could ascend at once; and on the sides of the
25 ladder were fastened all kinds of iron weapons. There
were swords, lances, hooks, daggers, so that if any one went
up carelessly or without looking upwards he was mangled
and his flesh caught on the weapons. And just beneath
the ladder was a dragon couching of wondrous size who
30 lay in wait for those going up and sought to frighten them
from going up. Now Saturus went up first, who had
given himself up for our sakes of his own accord, because
our faith had been of his own building, and he had not
been present when we were seized. And he reached the
35 top of the ladder, and turned, and said to me: ' Perpetua,

I await you; but see that the dragon bite you not.' And I said: ' In the name of Jesus Christ he will not hurt me.' And he put out his head gently, as if afraid of me, just at the foot of the ladder; and as though I were treading on the first step, I trod on his head. And I went up, and saw a vast expanse of garden, and in the midst a man sitting with white hair, in the dress of a shepherd, a tall man, milking sheep; and round about were many thousands clad in white. And he raised his head, and looked upon me, and said: ' You have well come, my child.' And he called me, and gave me a morsel of the milk which he was milking and I received it in my joined hands, and ate; and all they that stood around said: ' Amen.' And at the sound of the word I woke, still eating something sweet. And at once I told my brother, and we understood that we must suffer, and henceforward began to have no hope in this world.

V. After a few days a rumour ran that we were to be examined. Moreover, my father arrived from the city, worn with trouble, and came up the hill to see me, that he might overthrow my resolution, saying: ' Daughter, pity my white hairs! Pity your father, if I am worthy to be called father by you; if with these hands I have brought you up to this your prime of life, if I have preferred you to all your brothers! Give me not over to the reproach of men! Look upon your brothers, look upon your mother and your mother's sister, look upon your son who cannot live after you are gone! Lay aside your pride, do not ruin all of us, for none of us will ever speak freely again, if anything happen to you!' So spoke my father in his love for me, kissing my hands, and casting himself at my feet; and with tears called me by the name not of daughter but of lady. And I grieved for my father's sake, because he alone of all my kindred would not have joy in my suffering. And I comforted him, saying: ' It shall happen on that platform as God shall choose; for know well that we lie

not in our own power but in the power of God.' And
full of sorrow he left me.

VI. On another day when we were having our midday
meal, we were suddenly hurried off to be examined; and
5 we came to the market-place. Forthwith a rumour ran
through the neighbouring parts of the market-place, and
a vast crowd gathered. We went up on to the platform.
The others on being questioned confessed their faith. So
it came to my turn. And there was my father with my
10 child, and he drew me down from the step, beseeching me:
' Have pity on your baby.' And the procurator Hilarian,
who had then received the power of life and death in the
room of the late proconsul Minucius Timinianus, said
to me: ' Spare your father's white hairs; spare the tender
15 years of your child. Offer a sacrifice for the safety of the
Emperors.' And I answered: ' No.' ' Are you a Christian! ' said Hilarian. And I answered: ' I am.' And when
my father persisted in trying to overthrow my resolution,
he was ordered by Hilarian to be thrown down, and the
20 judge struck him with his rod. And I was grieved for
my father's plight, as if I had been struck myself, so did
I grieve for the sorrow that had come on his old age. Then
he passed sentence on the whole of us, and condemned us
to the beasts; and in great joy we went down into the
25 prison. Then because my baby was accustomed to take
the breast from me, and stay with me in prison, I sent at
once the deacon Pomponius to my father to ask for my baby.
But my father refused to give him. And as God willed,
neither had he any further wish for my breasts, nor did they
30 become inflamed ; that I might not be tortured by anxiety
for the baby and pain in my breasts.

VII. After a few days, while we were all praying,
suddenly in the middle of the prayer I spoke, and uttered
the name of Dinocrates; and I was astonished that he had
35 never come into mind till then; and I grieved thinking of

what had befallen him. And I saw at once that I was entitled, and ought, to make request for him. And I began to pray much for him, and make lamentation to the Lord. At once on this very night this was shown me. I saw Dinocrates coming forth from a dark place, where there were many other dark places, very hot and thirsty, his countenance pale and squalid; and the wound which he had when he died was in his face still. This Dinocrates had been my brother according to the flesh, seven years old, who had died miserably of a gangrene in the face, so that his death moved all to loathing. For him then I had prayed; and there was a great gulf between me and him, so that neither of us could approach the other. There was besides in the very place where Dinocrates was a font full of water, the rim of which was above the head of the child; and Dinocrates stood on tiptoe to drink. I grieved that the font should have water in it and that nevertheless he could not drink because of the height of the rim. And I woke and recognized that my brother was in trouble. But I trusted that I could relieve his trouble, and I prayed for him every day until we were transferred to the garrison prison, for we were to fight with the beasts at the garrison games on the Caesar Geta's birthday. And I prayed for him day and night with lamentations and tears that he might be given me.

VIII. During the daytime, while we stayed in the stocks, this was shown me. I saw that same place which I had seen before, and Dinocrates clean in body, well-clothed and refreshed; and where there had been a wound, I saw a scar; and the font which I had seen before had its rim lowered to the child's waist; and there poured water from it unceasingly; and on the rim a golden bowl full of water. And Dinocrates came forward and began to drink from it, and the bowl failed not. And when he had drunk enough of the water, he came forward being glad to play as children will. And I awoke. Then I knew that he had been released from punishment.

IX. Then after a few days Pudens the adjutant, who was in charge of the prison, who began to show us honour perceiving that there was some great power within us, began to admit many to see us, that both we and they might be refreshed by one another's company. Now when the day of the games approached, my father came in to me worn with trouble, and began to pluck out his beard and cast it on the ground, and to throw himself on his face, and to curse his years, and to say such words as might have turned the world upside down. I sorrowed for the unhappiness of his old age.

X. On the day before we were to fight, I saw in a vision Pomponius the deacon come hither to the door of the prison and knock loudly. And I went out to him, and opened to him. Now he was clad in a white robe without a girdle, wearing shoes curiously wrought. And he said to me: ' Perpetua, we are waiting for you; come.' And he took hold of my hand, and we began to pass through rough and broken country. Painfully and panting did we arrive at last at an amphitheatre, and he led me into the middle of the arena. And he said to me: ' Fear not; I am here with you, and I suffer with you.' And he departed. And I saw a huge crowd watching eagerly. And because I knew that I was condemned to the beasts, I marvelled that there were no beasts let loose on me. And there came out an Egyptian, foul of look, with his attendants to fight against me. And to me also there came goodly young men to be my attendants and supporters. And I was stripped and was changed into a man. And my supporters began to rub me down with oil, as they are wont to do before a combat; and I saw the Egyptian opposite rolling in the sand. And there came forth a man wondrously tall so that he rose above the top of the amphitheatre, clad in a purple

robe without a girdle with two stripes, one on either side,
running down the middle of the breast, and wearing shoes
curiously wrought made of gold and silver; carrying a
wand, like a trainer, and a green bough on which were
golden apples. And he asked for silence, and said: ' This 5
Egyptian, if he prevail over her, shall kill her with a
sword; and, if she prevail over him, she shall receive this
bough.' And he retired. And we came near to one another
and began to use our fists. My adversary wished to catch
hold of my feet, but I kept on striking his face with my 10
heels. And I was lifted up into the air, and began to strike
him in such fashion as would one that no longer trod on
earth. But when I saw that the fight lagged, I joined my
two hands, linking the fingers of the one with the fingers
of the other. And I caught hold of his head, and he fell 15
on his face; and I trod upon his head. And the people
began to shout, and my supporters to sing psalms. And I
came forward to the trainer, and received the bough. And
he kissed me, and said to me: ' Peace be with thee, my
daughter.' And I began to go in triumph to the Gate of Life. 20
And I awoke. And I perceived that I should not fight with
beasts but with the Devil; but I knew the victory to be
mine. Such were my doings up to the day before the
games. Of what was done in the games themselves let
him write who will."   25

XI. But the blessed Saturus also has made known this
vision of his own, which he has written out with his own
hand. " Methought we had suffered, and put off the
flesh, and began to be borne toward the east by four angels
whose hands touched us not. Now we moved not on our 30
backs looking upward, but as though we were climbing a
gentle slope. And when we were clear of the world below
we saw a great light, and I said to Perpetua, for she was
by my side: ' This is what the Lord promised us, we have
received His promise.' And while we were carried by 35

those four angels, we came upon a great open space, which was like as it might be a garden, having rose-trees and all kinds of flowers. The height of the trees was like the height of a cypress, whose leaves sang without ceasing.
5 Now there in the garden were certain four angels, more glorious than the others, who when they saw us, gave us honour, and said to the other angels: ' Lo! they are come; lo! they are come,' being full of wonder. And those four angels which bare us trembled and set us down, and we crossed
10 on foot a place strewn with violets, where we found Jucundus and Saturninus and Artaxius, who were burned alive in the same persecution, and Quintus who, being also a martyr, had died in the prison, and we asked of them where they were. The other angels said unto us: ' Come first
15 and enter and greet the Lord.'

XII. And we came near to a place whose walls were built like as it might be of light, and before the gate of that place were four angels standing, who as we entered clothed us in white robes. And we entered, and heard a
20 sound as of one voice saying: ' Holy, holy, holy,' without ceasing. And we saw sitting in the same place one like unto a man white-haired, having hair as white as snow, and with the face of a youth; whose feet we saw not. And on the right and on the left four elders; and behind them were
25 many other elders standing. And entering we stood in wonder before the throne; and the four angels lifted us up, and we kissed Him, and He stroked our faces with His hand. And the other elders said to us: ' Let us stand.' And we stood and gave the Kiss of Peace. And the elders
30 said to us: ' Go and play.' And I said to Perpetua: ' You have your wish.' And she said to me: ' Thanks be to God, that as I was merry in the flesh, so am I now still merrier here.'

XIII. And we went forth, and saw before the doors
35 Optatus the bishop on the right, and Aspasius the priest-

teacher on the left, severed and sad. And they cast themselves at our feet, and said: ' Make peace between us, for
you have gone forth, and left us thus.' And we said to
them: ' Are not you our father, and you our priest?'
Why should ye fall before our feet?' And we were 5
moved, and embraced them. And Perpetua began to talk
Greek with them, and we drew them aside into the garden
under a rose-tree. And while we talked with them, the
angels said to them: ' Let them refresh themselves; and
if ye have any quarrels among yourselves, forgive one 10
another.' And they put these to shame, and said to
Optatus: ' Reform your people, for they come to you
like men returning from the circus and contending about
its factions.' And it seemed to us as though they wished
to shut the gates. And we began to recognize many 15
brethren there, martyrs too amongst them. We were all
fed on a fragrance beyond telling, which contented us.
Then in my joy I awoke."

XIV. Such are the famous visions of the blessed martyrs
themselves, Saturus and Perpetua, which they wrote with 20
their own hands. As for Secundulus, God called him to
an earlier departure from this world while still in prison,
not without grace, that he might escape the beasts. Nevertheless his body, if not his soul, made acquaintance with
the sword. 25

XV. As for Felicitas indeed, she also was visited by the
grace of God in this wise. Being eight months gone with
child (for she was pregnant at the time of her arrest), as
the day for the spectacle drew near she was in great sorrow
for fear lest because of her pregnancy her martyrdom 30
should be delayed, since it is against the law for women
with child to be exposed for punishment, and lest she
should shed her sacred and innocent blood among others
afterwards who were malefactors. Her fellow-martyrs too
were deeply grieved at the thought of leaving so good a 35

comrade and fellow-traveller behind alone on the way to
the same hope. So in one flood of common lamentation
they poured forth a prayer to the Lord two days before the
games. Immediately after the prayer her pains came upon
5 her. And since from the natural difficulty of an eight-
months' labour she suffered much in child-birth, one of the
warders said to her: 'You who so suffer now, what will
you do when you are flung to the beasts which, when you
refused to sacrifice, you despised?' And she answered:
10 'Now I suffer what I suffer: but then Another will be
in me who will suffer for me, because I too am to suffer
for Him.' So she gave birth to a girl, whom one of the
sisters brought up as her own daughter.

XVI. Since, therefore, the Holy Spirit has permitted,
15 and by permitting willed, the story of the games themselves
to be written, we cannot choose but carry out, however
unworthy to supplement so glorious a history, the injunction,
or rather sacred bequest, of the most holy Perpetua, adding at
the same time one example of her steadfastness and loftiness
20 of soul. When they were treated with unusual rigour by the
commanding officer because his fears were aroused through
the warnings of certain foolish people that they might be
carried off from prison by some magic spells, she challenged
him to his face: 'Why do you not at least suffer us to refresh
25 ourselves, " the most noble " among the condemned, belonging as we do to Caesar and chosen to fight on his birthday? Or is it not to your credit that we should appear there-
on in better trim?' The commanding officer trembled
and blushed; and so ordered them to be used more kindly,
30 giving her brothers and other persons leave to visit, that
they might refresh themselves in their company. By this
time the governor of the prison was himself a believer.

XVII. Moreover, on the day before the games when
they celebrated that last supper, called 'the free festivity',
35 not as a 'festivity', but, so far as they could make it so,

a ' love-feast ', with the same steadfastness they flung words
here and there among the people, threatening them with
the judgement of God, calling to witness the happiness of
their own passion, laughing at the inquisitiveness of the
crowd. Said Saturus: ' To-morrow does not satisfy you, 5
for what you hate you love to see. Friends to-day, foes
to-morrow. Yet mark our faces well, that when the day
comes you may know us again.' So all left the place
amazed, and many of them became believers.

XVIII. The day of their victory dawned, and they 10
proceeded from the prison to the amphitheatre, as if they
were on their way to heaven, with gay and gracious looks;
trembling, if at all, not with fear but joy. Perpetua
followed with shining steps, as the true wife of Christ, as
the darling of God, abashing with the high spirit in her 15
eyes the gaze of all ; Felicitas also, rejoicing that she had
brought forth in safety that so she might fight the beasts,
from blood to blood, from midwife to gladiator, to find
in her Second Baptism her child-birth washing. And when
they were led within the gate, and were on the point of 20
being forced to put on the dress, the men of the priests of
Saturn, the women of those dedicated to Ceres, the noble
Perpetua resisted steadfastly to the last. For she said:
' Therefore we came to this issue of our own free will, that
our liberty might not be violated; therefore we pledged 25
our lives, that we might do no such thing: this was our
pact with you.' Injustice acknowledged justice ; the commanding officer gave permission that they should enter the
arena in their ordinary dress as they were. Perpetua was
singing a psalm of triumph, as already treading on the 30
head of the Egyptian. Revocatus, Saturninus, and Saturus
were threatening the onlookers with retribution ; when
they came within sight of Hilarian, they began to signify
to him by nods and gestures: ' Thou art judging us, but
God shall judge thee.' The people infuriated thereat 35

demanded that they should be punished with scourging before a line of beast-fighters. And they for this at least gave one another joy, that they had moreover won some share in the sufferings of their Lord.

5   XIX. But He who had said: ' Ask and ye shall receive ' had granted to those who asked Him that death which each had craved. For, whenever they talked amongst themselves about their hopes of martyrdom, Saturninus declared that he wished to be cast to all the beasts; so indeed would he 10 wear a more glorious crown. Accordingly at the outset of the show he was matched with the leopard and recalled from him; he was also (later) mauled on the platform by the bear. Saturus on the other hand had a peculiar dread of the bear, but counted beforehand on being dispatched 15 by one bite of the leopard. And so when he was offered to the wild boar, the fighter with beasts, who had bound him to the boar, was gored from beneath by the same beast, and died after the days of the games were over, whereas Saturus was only dragged. And when he was tied up on 20 the bridge before the bear, the bear refused to come out of his den. So Saturus for the second time was recalled unhurt.

XX. For the young women the Devil made ready a mad heifer, an unusual animal selected for this reason, 25 that he wished to match their sex with that of the beast. And so after being stripped and enclosed in nets they were brought into the arena. The people were horrified, beholding in the one a tender girl, in the other a woman fresh from child-birth, with milk dripping from her breasts. 30 So they were recalled and dressed in tunics without girdles. Perpetua was tossed first, and fell on her loins. Sitting down she drew back her torn tunic from her side to cover her thighs, more mindful of her modesty than of her suffering. Then having asked for a pin she further fastened 35 her disordered hair. For it was not seemly that a martyr

should suffer with her hair dishevelled, lest she should seem
to mourn in the hour of her glory. Then she rose, and
seeing that Felicitas was bruised, approached, gave a hand
to her, and lifted her up. And the two stood side by side,
and the cruelty of the people being now appeased, they 5
were recalled to the Gate of Life. There Perpetua was
supported by a certain Rusticus, then a catechumen, who
kept close to her; and being roused from what seemed like
sleep, so completely had she been in the Spirit and in
ecstasy, began to look about her, and said to the amaze- 10
ment of all : ' When we are to be thrown to that heifer,
I cannot tell.' When she heard what had already taken
place, she refused to believe it till she had observed certain
marks of ill-usage on her body and dress. Then she summoned her brother and spoke to him and the catechumen, 15
saying: ' Stand ye all fast in the faith, and love one another; and be not offended by our sufferings.'

XXI. Saturus also at another gate was encouraging the
soldier Pudens: ' In a word ', said he, ' what I counted on
and foretold has come to pass, not a beast so far has touched 20
me. And now, that you may trust me wholeheartedly,
see, I go forth yonder, and with one bite of the leopard all
is over.' And forthwith, as the show was ending, the
leopard was let loose, and with one bite Saturus was so
drenched in blood that the people as he came back shouted 25
in attestation of his Second Baptism, ' Bless you, well
bathed! Bless you, well bathed! ' Blessed indeed was he
who had bathed after this fashion. Then he said to the
soldier Pudens: ' Farewell! Keep my faith and me in
mind! And let these things not confound, but confirm 30
you.' And with that he asked for the ring from Pudens's
finger, plunged it in his own wound, and gave it back as
a legacy, bequeathing it for a pledge and memorial of his
blood. Then by this time lifeless he was flung with the
rest on to the place allotted to the throat-cutting. And 35

when the people asked for them to be brought into the open, that, when the sword pierced their bodies, these might lend their eyes for partners in the murder, they rose unbidden and made their way whither the people
5 willed, after first kissing one another, that they might perfect their martyrdom with the rite of the Pax. The rest without a movement in silence received the sword, Saturus in deeper silence, who, as he had been the first to climb the ladder, was the first to give up the ghost; for
10 now as then he awaited Perpetua. Perpetua, however, that she might taste something of the pain, was struck on the bone and cried out, and herself guided to her throat the wavering hand of the young untried gladiator. Perhaps so great a woman, who was feared by the unclean spirit,
15 could not otherwise be slain except she willed.

O valiant and blessed martyrs! O truly called and chosen to the glory of Jesus Christ our Lord! He who magnifies, honours, and adores that glory should recite to the edification of the Church these examples also, not less
20 precious at least than those of old; that so new instances of virtue may testify that one and the self-same Spirit is working to this day with the Father, God Almighty, and with His Son Jesus Christ our Lord, to whom belong splendour and power immeasurable for ever and ever.
25 Amen.

VII

ACTS OF S. CYPRIAN

(SEPTEMBER 14, A.D. 258)

THESE Acts constitute one of the best examples of that class of Acts which is founded on official reports. They consist (v. Delehaye, *Legends of the Saints*, p. 112) of three separate documents, (1) the first interrogatory, (2) the arrest and second interrogatory, (3) the martyrdom, which are strung together by a few connecting phrases of the editor.

Cyprian was a rich man, well known in Carthage as an orator and pleader. Two years after his conversion he was made Bishop of Carthage (A. D. 248). Two years later the Decian persecution began. At the beginning of the persecution Cyprian retired from Carthage into hiding, as his presence was an additional danger to his flock, and it was of supreme importance that he should live to watch over them. It would have been as impossible in Carthage as it was in Rome on the martyrdom of S. Fabian to elect a successor ; but he was reproached by his enemies, and particularly by the Roman priests who contrasted his conduct with S. Fabian's. Decius was killed in the field in A.D. 251. The reign of his successor, Gallus, was marked by an appalling plague, of which the Christians, and Cyprian in particular, took advantage to care for and nurse their persecutors. In 257, three years after the accession of Valerian, the persecution was renewed after three years' peace, but at first punishment was limited to exile. Cyprian was arrested and sent into exile as narrated in the Acta. On the night of his arrival at Curubis (September 14, 257) Cyprian had, before he had quite fallen asleep, a vision (*Life by Pontius*, ch. xii). He saw a young man of superhuman stature, who led him to the Praetorium. The proconsul was writing in his tablets. The young man did not speak, but, by spreading out his hand flat like the blade of a sword, indicated the stroke of the executioner. Cyprian asked for a day's reprieve to arrange his affairs, especially the affairs of the Church. The young man, by twisting his fingers, one behind another, conveyed to him that the request for a day's reprieve was granted by the proconsul. The day signified a year, for his passion took place that day year.

In July 258 Cyprian was recalled from exile. Valerian had issued a more severe edict that bishops, priests, and deacons were to be executed at once. Cyprian was advised to fly, but refused. He hid, however, for the moment, to avoid a summons to Utica, where the proconsul then was, for he wished, as he told his flock in the last of his letters, to die at Carthage in his own city. He would return to Carthage as soon as the proconsul returned thither.

When Galerius went back to Carthage, Cyprian was there according to his promise. Then followed the arrest and its sequel as recorded in the Acts. Some additional details are given in his life by Pontius, one of his deacons. He went to his death ' with a high and resolute spirit, in his face cheerfulness, in his heart fortitude '. He spent his last night in comfort, supping with Pontius and his friends. The 14th dawned, ' the day singled out of all days, the day of promise, the day of God.' It was sunny and cloudless, ' rejoicing in the thought of its martyr.' There was an immense crowd of Christians, like an army ' bent on taking death by storm '. Cyprian arrived weary and drenched with sweat after his long journey. An official, who had once been a Christian, offered him a change of garments. Cyprian refused, ' That would be to cure a trouble, which before the day ends may be over.' He was escorted by officers and a guard. The scene of his martyrdom was a level space surrounded by woods. Many of the spectators climbed into the trees. The executioner was unnerved, his fingers could scarcely grasp the sword. The centurion on duty took his place, and ' strength being given to him from on high' won for the great bishop his crown of martyrdom.

S. Cyprian was a great bishop, a great administrator. He is famous as a writer for his letters and for the short treatise *On the Unity of the Catholic Church*. With the exception of Tertullian he is the first great Latin Christian writer. Equally famous is his controversy with the followers of Novatian, the rigorists who wished to refuse all hope of reconciliation, even at death, to the lapsed ; and, even more, his other controversy with Pope Stephen, in which he maintained the necessity of the rebaptism of those baptized by heretics, and, incidentally, raised the question of the position of the Bishop of Rome in relation to other bishops. The quarrel with Pope Stephen was never healed, but peace seems to have been re-established with his successor Xystus, and harmony between the Churches of Rome and Carthage resumed before the death of Cyprian.

Text in KNOPF *from* HARTEL

I. 1. DURING the consulship of the Emperors Valerian and Gallienus, Valerian being consul for the fourth and Gallienus for the third time, on August 30 at Carthage in his private room Paternus the proconsul said to Cyprian the bishop : 'The most sacred Emperors Valerian and Gallienus 5 have thought fit to send me a letter, in which they have commanded that those who do not observe the Roman religion must recognize the Roman rites. I have therefore made inquiries concerning yourself. What answer have you to give me ? '   10

2. Cyprian the bishop said : 'I am a Christian and a bishop. I know no other God but the One True God, who "made heaven and earth, the sea, and all that in them is". This God we Christians serve, to Him we pray day and night for ourselves, and for all men, and for 15 the safety of the Emperors themselves.'

3. The proconsul Paternus said : 'Is your will constant in this ? '

Cyprian the bishop answered : 'A good will, which knows God, cannot be altered.'   20

4. The proconsul Paternus said : 'Can you then in accordance with the order of Valerius and Gallienus go into exile to the city of Curubis ? '

Cyprian the bishop said : 'I will go.'

5. The proconsul Paternus said : 'They have thought 25 fit to write to me not about bishops only, but also about priests. I would know therefore from you who the priests are, who reside in this city.'

Cyprian the bishop answered : 'It is an excellent and beneficial provision of your laws that informers are 30 forbidden. They cannot therefore be revealed and reported by me. They will be found in their own cities.'

6. The proconsul Paternus said : ' I will seek them out here to-day.'

5   Cyprian the bishop said : 'Since our discipline forbids any one to offer himself unsought, and this is also at variance with your principles, they cannot offer themselves any more than I can report them ; but if sought out by you they will be found.'

10   7. The proconsul Paternus said : ' They shall be found by me.' And added : ' The emperors have also given instructions that in no place shall meetings be held, nor shall any enter the cemeteries. If therefore any fail to observe these beneficial instructions, he shall suffer death.'

15   Cyprian the bishop answered : ' Do as you are instructed.'

II. 1. Then the proconsul Paternus ordered the blessed Cyprian to be banished. And as he stayed long time in exile, the proconsul Aspasius Paternus was succeeded in the proconsulship by Galerius Maximus, who ordered

20 the holy bishop Cyprian to be recalled from banishment and brought before him.

2. When Cyprian, the holy martyr chosen by God had returned from the city Curubis, which had been assigned as his place of banishment by command of Aspasius then

25 proconsul, by divine command he remained in his own gardens, whence he daily expected to be summoned, as had been shown him. 3. While he still lingered in that place, suddenly on September 13 in the consulship of Tuscus and Bassus there came to him two high officials,

30 one an equerry of the staff of the proconsul Galerius Maximus, and the other a member of the same staff, an equerry of the bodyguard. 4. These lifted him into a carriage, placed him between them, and conveyed him to the house of Sextus, whither the proconsul Galerius

35 Maximus had retired to recover his health.

5. And so the same Galerius Maximus the proconsul ordered Cyprian to be remanded till the morrow. For the time being blessed Cyprian withdrew under guard to the house of a high official, equerry on the same staff of the illustrious Galerius Maximus the proconsul, and remained 5 with him at his house in the street which is called Saturn's between the temple of Venus and the temple of Public Welfare. There the whole congregation of the brethren gathered: when this came to holy Cyprian's knowledge he gave orders that charge should be kept of the young women, 10 for all had remained in the street before the door of the official's house.

III. 1. On the morrow, being September 14, a great crowd gathered in the morning to the house of Sextus in accordance with the command of Galerius Maximus the 15 proconsul. 2. And so the same Galerius Maximus the proconsul ordered that Cyprian the bishop should be brought before him on the morrow where he sat in the Hall Sauciolum. 3. When he had been brought before him, Galerius Maximus the proconsul said to Cyprian the 20 bishop : ' Are you Thascius Cyprianus ? '

Cyprian the bishop answered : ' I am.'

4. Galerius Maximus the proconsul said : ' Have you taken on yourself to be Pope of persons holding sacrilegious opinions ? '   25

Cyprian the bishop answered : ' Yes.'

5. Galerius Maximus the proconsul said : ' The most sacred Emperors have commanded you to perform the rite.'

Cyprian the bishop answered : ' I refuse.'   30

6. Galerius Maximus the proconsul said : ' Consider your own interest.'

Cyprian the bishop answered : ' Do as you are bid. In so clear a case there is no need for consideration.'

IV. 1. Galerius Maximus having conferred with the 35

council gave sentence hardly and reluctantly in these
terms : ' You have long lived in the holding of sacrilegious
opinions, and have joined with yourself very many members of an abominable conspiracy, and have set yourself up
5 as an enemy of the gods of Rome and religious ordinances,
nor have the pious and most sacred Emperors Valerian
and Gallienus, the Augusti, and Valerian, the most noble
Caesar, been able to recall you to the observance of their
rites. 2. And therefore since you have been convicted as
10 the contriver and standard-bearer in most atrocious crimes,
you shall be an example to those whom by your wickedness
you have joined with you : discipline shall be vindicated
in your blood.' 3. With these words he read from his
tablets the sentence : ' It is our pleasure that Thascius
15 Cyprianus should be executed by the sword.'

Cyprian the bishop said : ' Thanks be to God ! '

V. 1. After this sentence the crowd of brethren cried :
' Let us also be beheaded with him.' Hence arose an up-
roar among the brethren, and a great crowd accompanied
20 him. 2. So the same Cyprian was led forth on to the land
of Sextus, and there he divested himself of his mantle, and
kneeled upon the ground, and bowed in prayer to the
Lord. 3. And when he had divested himself of his dalmatic and handed it to the deacons, he stood clad in his
25 linen garment, and prepared to await the executioner.
4. When the executioner arrived he charged his friends
that they should give to the same executioner twenty-five
golden pieces. Napkins and handkerchiefs were strewn
before him by the brethren. 5. Thereafter blessed Cyprian
30 bound his eyes with his own hand, but, as he could not
fasten the ends of the handkerchief for himself, the priest
Julianus and Julianus the sub-deacon fastened them for
him.

6. So the blessed Cyprian suffered, and his body was
35 laid out hard by to content the curiosity of the heathen.

Thence it was removed by night, and, accompanied by
tapers and torches, was conducted with prayers in great
triumph to the burial-ground of Macrobius Candidianus
the procurator, which lies on the Mappalian way near the
fishponds. A few days later Galerius Maximus the pro- 5
consul died.

VI. The most blessed martyr Cyprian suffered on the
14th day of September under the Emperors Valerian and
Gallienus, in the reign of our Lord Jesus Christ, to whom
belong honour and glory for ever and ever. Amen.   10

VIII

ACTS OF SS. FRUCTUOSUS AND HIS DEACONS

(JANUARY 21, A. D. 259)

FRUCTUOSUS was Bishop of Tarragona in Spain, martyred on
January 21, 259, during the reign of Valerian and Gallienus.
S. Augustine (*b.* A. D. 354) speaks of him and his companions
in *Sermon* 273, having certainly the *Acta* before him. Prudentius,
the famous Christian poet (*b.* A. D. 348), celebrates them in his
6th *Hymn* (*Peristeph.*), following the account in the *Acta* very
closely. Some quotations both from him and from S. Augustine
will be found in the notes. Their day is January 21.

Text from RUINART, *Acta Mart.*, p. 264

I. DURING the reign of Valerian and Gallienus, in the
consulship of Aemilian and Bassus on Sunday the 16th of
January Fructuosus the bishop and the deacons Augurius
and Eulogius were arrested. Fructuosus the bishop having
5 retired to his bedchamber, certain orderlies, Aurelius,
Festucius, Aelius, Pollentius, Donatus, and Maximus made
their way to his house. When he heard the sound of their
feet, he at once arose, and went out to meet them in his
slippers. The soldiers said to him : ' Come, the governor
10 summons you and your deacons.'

Fructuosus the bishop said : ' Let us go. If you do not
mind, I will put on my shoes.'

The soldiers answered : ' Put on your shoes, and welcome.'

15 Soon after their arrival, they were lodged in prison.
Fructuosus resolute, rejoicing in the crown of the Lord,
to which he had been called, prayed without ceasing. With
him were the brethren, cheering him and beseeching him
to keep them in mind.

20 II. On the next day he baptized our brother, called
Rogatian, in prison. They spent six days in prison, and

on Friday the 21st of January they were produced in court and given audience. Aemilian the governor said : ' Admit Fructuosus the bishop, and Augurius and Eulogius.'

The officials said : ' They are in court.'

Aemilian the governor said to Fructuosus the bishop: 5 ' Have you heard what the Emperors have ordered? '

Fructuosus the bishop answered : ' I do not know what they have ordered. I however am a Christian.'

Aemilian the governor said : ' They have ordered that the gods be worshipped.' 10

Fructuosus the bishop said : ' I worship one God, who " made heaven and earth, the sea and all that in them is ".'.

Aemilian said : ' Do you know that there are gods? '

Fructuosus the bishop answered : ' I know no such thing.' 15

Aemilian said : ' You shall know later.'

Fructuosus the bishop looked unto the Lord, and began to pray within himself.

Aemilian the governor said : ' Who are obeyed, who are feared, who are adored, if the gods are not worshipped, nor 20 the countenances of the Emperors adored? '

Aemilian the governor said to Augurius the deacon : ' Pay no heed to the words of Fructuosus.'

Augurius the deacon answered : ' I worship God the Almighty.' 25

Aemilian the governor said to Eulogius the deacon : ' Do you worship Fructuosus also? '

Eulogius the deacon answered : ' I do not worship Fructuosus; but I worship Him whom Fructuosus also worships.' 30

Aemilian the governor said to Fructuosus the bishop : ' Are you a bishop? '

Fructuosus the bishop answered : ' I am.'

Aemilian said : ' You were.' And he gave sentence that they should be burnt alive. 35

III. When Fructuosus the bishop was being led with his deacons to the amphitheatre, the people began to condole with Fructuosus the bishop, for he was greatly beloved not only by the brethren but by the heathen also. For he
5 was such a man as the Holy Spirit by the mouth of Blessed Paul the Apostle, the vessel of election, the teacher of the Gentiles declared a bishop ought to be. Wherefore also the brethren, who knew him to be on his way to so great glory, rejoiced rather than grieved. And when many out
10 of brotherly love offered them a cup of drugged wine to drink, he said : 'The hour for breaking our fast is not yet come.' For the day was in its fourth hour. Now on Wednesday they had solemnly held a fast in the prison. So on Friday he hastened joyful and free from care, that
15 he might break his fast with the Martyrs and the Prophets in the Paradise which the Lord has prepared for them that love Him.

When he reached the amphitheatre, immediately there came to him one called Augustalis, his Reader, beseeching
20 him with tears to be allowed to loose his shoes. The blessed martyr answered him : 'Let that be, my Son : I will loose my shoes myself, bold and joyful and assured of the promise of the Lord.'

When he had loosed his shoes, then came to him our
25 brother and fellow-soldier, Felix by name, and clasped his right hand, beseeching him to be mindful of him. To whom the holy Fructuosus answered in a loud voice in all men's hearing : 'I must have in mind the Catholic Church, which is dispersed from the East even unto the
30 West.'

IV. And so being set in the gate of the amphitheatre, he was now on the point of approach to what was less an agony than an unfading crown. The orderlies of the court, whose names are given above, were on the watch;
35 yet in a voice that our brethren themselves could hear

Fructuosus the bishop said, under the guidance and indeed
in the words of the Holy Spirit : ' Ye shall not long lack
a shepherd, nor shall the love and promise of the Lord fail
you either here or hereafter. For this on which ye look
seems the infirmity of an hour.' So when he had com- 5
forted the brethren, they entered on the way of salvation,
being worthy and fortunate in their very martyrdom that
they enjoyed the fruit of the Holy Scriptures according
to promise. For they were like Ananias, Azarias, and
Misael, so that in them also the Divine Trinity was 10
visible; to each at his station in the fire the Father was
present, the Son gave succour, for each the Holy Spirit
walked in the midst of the fire. And when the bands were
burnt, with which their hands had been fastened, mindful
of the Divine prayer and of their usual custom, they fell 15
on their knees, rejoicing and assured of resurrection, and,
extending their arms as a symbol of the Lord's victory,
prayed to the Lord till they gave up their souls together.

V. Thereafter the usual wonderful acts of the Lord
were not wanting, and the heaven opened before the eyes of 20
Babylas and Mygdonius our brethren, who were members
of the household of Aemilian the governor. These also
showed to the daughter of the same Aemilian, their mistress according to the flesh, holy Fructuosus the bishop
with his deacons, the stakes still left to which they had 25
been bound, ascending to Heaven crowned. And they summoned Aemilian saying : ' Come and behold those whom
you have to-day condemned how they have been restored
to heaven and to their hope.' But, when Aemilian came,
he was not worthy to behold them. 30

VI. The brethren sad, as those left without a shepherd,
were burdened with sorrow; not that they grieved for
Fructuosus, but rather missed him, remembering the faith
of each, and his contest. On the following night they came
with haste to the amphitheatre, bearing wine with which 35

to quench the smouldering bodies. This done each col-
lected the ashes of the same martyrs, as he was able, and
claimed them for his own. But neither in this were the
wonders of our Lord and Saviour wanting to increase the
5 faith of believers and to give a sign to His little ones. For
it behoved Fructuosus the martyr to confirm afterwards
in his own passion and bodily resurrection that which in his
teaching when in the world he had promised by God's mercy
in our Lord and Saviour. Therefore after his passion he
10 appeared to the brethren, and charged them that what each
had taken of the ashes out of love they should restore
without delay, and should see to their burial together in
one place.

VII. [To Aemilian also who had condemned them
15 Fructuosus showed himself with his deacons in the robes
of promise, chiding and mocking him, and saying that it
availed him nought to have vainly believed that they were
robbed of their bodies and laid in earth, since he saw them
now in glory.] O Blessed Martyrs, who were proved in
20 the fire like precious gold, clad in the breastplate of faith
and the helmet of salvation, who have been crowned with
a diadem and crown that fadeth not away, because they
trod underfoot the head of the devil! O Blessed Martyrs,
who have earned a worthy habitation in the Heavens,
25 standing at the right-hand of Christ, blessing God the
Father Almighty and our Lord Jesus Christ His Son!
The Lord has received His Martyrs in peace for their
good confession, to whom belong honour and glory for
ever and ever. Amen.

IX

PASSION OF SS. JAMES AND MARIAN

(MAY 6, A. D. 259)

MARIAN (Marianus) and James were martyred in the reign of Valerian. His first edict was issued in August A. D. 257. It was directed against persons in Holy Orders, bishops, priests, and deacons only. Bishops were removed from their sees, Cyprian, for instance, was sent to Curubis (*Acts of S. Cyprian*, ch. i, p. 95), nine bishops of Numidia were condemned to the mines at Sigus near Cirta, others, among whom were Agapius and Secundinus, were banished; all assemblies for worship were forbidden, and all access to the cemeteries where worship usually took place. Any one who transgressed this last provision was to be punished with death. Private Christian worship was not forbidden. His second edict (or 'rescript') was issued in July, A. D. 258, under this all bishops, priests, and deacons were to be punished at once (with death); senators and knights and men of rank were to lose dignity and be deprived of their property, and, if they still persisted in their confession of Christianity, were to be put to death; Christian matrons were to be deprived of their property and banished; employees on imperial estates, who were a large body, were to be sent in chains to Caesar's farms. It was a stroke directed against the Christian leaders, clerical and lay, and against Christian worship, and intended at the same time to cut off their monetary supplies and enrich the State.

At Rome the bodies of S. Peter and S. Paul were removed for safety from their tombs on the Vatican and the Ostian way to the Catacombs on the Appian way; Pope Sixtus II was martyred on August 6, and Tarsicius, an acolyte who was bearing the Blessed Sacrament, was beaten to death rather than betray ' that heavenly Body to mad dogs '. Cyprian (v. p. 99) was martyred in Africa on September 14, A. D. 258, Fructuosus (v. p. 103) in Spain on January 21, A. D. 259, the Bishops Agapius and Secundinus with Tertulla and Antonia (ch. xi) on April 30, Marian and James on May 6.

S. Augustine celebrates them in *Sermon* 284, referring

especially to the mother of Marian (ch. xiii), 'Not for nothing was she called Mary.'

The Passion of SS. James and Marian is authentic and contemporary. Its account exactly fits the facts :

1. Agapius and Secundinus are returning from exile inflicted under the first edict. They are martyred under the provisions of the second.

2. The author of the account is examined (ch. iv), but, not being one of the higher clergy, released.

3. Marian is tortured (nothing was said of torture in the edicts) for a special reason, he had confessed to be a reader, and the authorities wrongly suspected that he was concealing the fact that he was a deacon, like James (ch. v).

4. Aemilian is a knight. He is already in prison (ch. viii) under a confession of Christianity : on persisting in this he is put to death.

Throughout the author assumes the knowledge of the edicts, as contemporary events. His own examination and release in ch. iv, though clear to those to whom he was writing, would be completely obscure to us if we did not know the facts from other sources.

There remain the cases of Tertulla and Antonia (ch. xi), and of the lay people (ch. x).

Tertulla and Antonia were probably condemned under the first edict for attending public assemblies for worship.

The lay people may have suffered under the same charge, but Sign. Pio Franchi de' Cavalieri (*Studi e Testi*, iii. 18) reminds us that this was in Numidia, an unquiet province, exposed just at this time, as we learn from inscriptions, to continual attacks and insurrections. The Government, he suggests, probably thought the Christians had stirred up the barbarians, or the malcontents, or even that there was a regular understanding between them. The numbers of the laity suggest some such cause.   *Text from* GEBHARDT, p. 134

I. 1. WHENEVER the blessed martyrs of God Almighty and His Christ, as they hasten to their promised kingdom in heaven, give with diffidence some charge to their dear ones, mindful of the humility which is ever wont to exalt men in the Faith, the more modestly they make their request the more surely they obtain it.

2. To me also this duty of proclaiming their glory has been left by God's illustrious witnesses, I mean Marian (Marianus), one of our beloved brethren, and James, both 5 of whom you know to have been closely twined with me, not only by the common bond of the Gospel, but also by fellowship in life and private ties. 3. Who, when about to wage so lofty a contest against the distresses of an age so cruel and heathen onslaughts, charged that their warfare 10 on which they entered by the impulse of the Spirit should through me come to the knowledge of the brethren, not that they wished the glory of their crown to be boastfully proclaimed on earth, but that the multitude of common folk and the people of God might be armed by the trials 15 of the past to be examples of the Faith. 4. And it was not without reason that they laid upon me in the confidence of friendship that task which I am about to fulfil. For who can question the fellowship of our life in peace, when the same season of persecution has found us living in unbroken love? 20

II. 1. For we were proceeding to Numidia together, as ever before, and had entered, a company of friends and equals, on that journey which was leading me to the welcome duties imposed by faith and religion, them to Heaven.

2. We had reached a place called Muguae, the suburb 25 of the colony of Cirta, a city where at that moment through the blind fury of the heathen and the action of the military officials the onslaughts of persecution surged like waves of this present world, and the rage of the destroying Devil gaped with greedy jaws to try the faith 30 of the just. Henceforward the blessed martyrs Marian and James were in possession of sure signs that the Divine choice had fallen on them, for, having been led when the hour was ripe into that district in which the storm of persecution was raging with unusual fierceness, they 35

understood that their steps had been directed under
Christ's guidance to the very place of their crown. 4. For
the fury of a bloodstained and blinded governor hating and
working hatred was hunting out with bands of soldiers all
5 the beloved of God.

5. Nor was the frenzy of his cruelty wreaked on those
alone who, undisturbed by previous persecutions, were
living unto God without let or hindrance, but against
these also the Devil stretched forth his insatiate hand,
10 who were long ago driven into exile, martyrs in spirit,
if not yet in blood; on these the savage madness of the
governor had bestowed their crown.

III. 1. Among these there were being conducted from
their exile to the governor Agapius and Secundinus,
15 bishops worthy to be praised, both for their concord in the
love of the Spirit, one for the added holiness of celibacy.
2. They were being conducted, I say, not, as the heathen
thought, from punishment to punishment, but rather from
glory to glory, from one contest to another, that those who
20 by upholding the Name of Christ had subdued the lying
pomps of the world might also by virtue of a faith made
perfect tread underfoot the sting of death. 3. For it was
not lawful they should seek victory more tardily in an
earthly struggle, whom the Master already was in haste
25 to have with Himself. 4. And during that journey,
wherein Agapius and Secundinus, famous bishops turned into
glorious martyrs, proceeded, by the election of Christ as
well as by the temporal order of the governor, to the combat
of their blessed passion, it befell, brethren, that they deigned
30 to enter our lodging. And so mighty a spirit of quickening
and of grace was in them that it was not enough for God's
holy and illustrious witnesses to devote their own precious
blood to glorious martyrdom unless by the inspiration of
their faith they made others martyrs also. 6. So strong was
35 their charity, so strong their love to the brethren, that,

though they might have silently built up the faith of the
brotherhood by examples of such faithful and stubborn
fortitude, nevertheless, making wider provision for the
steadfastness of our perseverance, they poured into our
hearts the dew of sound discourse; for those who lived on 5
the word of God could not keep silence. 7. No wonder
that in those few days the souls of all of us were stirred to
fuller life by the wholesome discourse of those in whom
Christ already shone in loveliness flashing from their
coming passion. 10

IV. 1. Finally, in their departure they left Marian and
James so disposed by their example and teaching that these
were ready to follow the guidance of the fresh footprints
of their glory. 2. For hardly had two days slipped away
before their own palms summoned our beloved Marian 15
and James. 3. For here it was not a case of one or two
police, as in other places, but a furious bevy of centurions
and a disorderly crowd had flocked to the country-house
where we lived as though it were some famous seat of the
Faith. 4. Welcome inroad! Blessed tumult, a theme for 20
joy. For they came to us only for this that the righteous
blood of Marian and James might ratify God's choice.
5. Scarcely could I, brothers beloved, keep in bounds at
that moment my overflowing joy—I who two days before
had sent some from my arms to the very last act of their 25
passion, and kept others, martyrs to come, with me still.
6. When the ripe hour of the Divine choice made a louder
call on those, it touched me also with some portion of my
brothers' glory, and I was dragged from Muguae to the
colony of Cirta. 7. I was followed by my dear friends, 30
elect to the palm of suffering, who were guided by their
love for me and the choice, now already ripe, of Christ.
8. So strangely but in perfect order of march those followed
who were destined to go before. 9. In the end they had
not long to wait; for, while encouraging me with special 35

fervour, they betrayed by the frankness of their joy that they were Christians. 10. Soon, when questioned, as they persisted in bold confession of the Name, they were conducted to prison.

5   V. 1. Then they were assailed with many severe tortures by the police, those executioners of just and pious souls, who had called in to aid them in their cruelty a centurion and the magistrates of Cirta, the Devil's priests, as if faith, which sets no store by the care of the body, 10 could be broken by the mangling of the limbs. 2. And James, indeed, always by virtue of his faith stricter than most, who had already once triumphed over the attacks of the Decian persecution, was at pains to confess himself not a Christian only, but a deacon. 3. Thereby he exposed 15 Marian to the tortures, because he only confessed to being a reader, as indeed he was.

4. What tortures were those! What novelty in the torments! How cunningly devised by the poisonous intelligence of the Devil, and the arts by which he turns men 20 from the faith. 5. Marian was hung up to be torn; to that martyr in the very midst of his mangling grace was given; he was so tortured that the very pain exalted him. 6. The thongs that held him as he hung bound, not his hands, but the top joints of his thumbs, that these, from 25 their slightness and weakness, might suffer more in supporting the rest of the limbs. 7. Moreover, unequal weights were fastened to his feet, that the whole framework of the body, torn two ways at once by contending agonies, and broken by the tearing of the bowels, might hang by 30 its sinews. 8. You were of no avail, heathen wickedness, against the temple of God, against the joint heir with Christ! 9. Though you hung up his limbs, racked his sides, rent his bowels, my Marian, trusting in God, grew in spirit as much as he grew in body. 10. At last the cruelty of his torturers 35 was beaten, and much rejoicing in his triumph he was

shut up again in prison. There with James and the rest of the brethren he celebrated the joy of the victory of the Lord in repeated prayer.

VI. 1. How now, ye heathen? Do ye believe that Christians, whom the joy of the everlasting light awaits, 5 feel the pains of prison and shrink from the darkness of this world? 2. The Spirit, in sure hope of the coming reward, embracing heaven in its thought, has no further part in its own sufferings. 3. Though you seek out for punishment an abode secret and hidden, the oppressive 10 horror of some murky cavern, the home of darkness, those who trust in God feel no place hideous, no time gloomy. 4. Christ cherishes by night and day them, His brethren, dedicate to God His Father. 5. For what the favour of God showed to Marian for assurance of the hope 15 of salvation, when after that torturing of his body he had sunk deep into the calm of slumber, he himself on his awaking told us, in these words: 6. ' There was shown me, brethren, the towering front of a tribunal high and white, on which instead of the governor there sat a judge 20 fair to look upon. 7. In that place there was a scaffold, whose floor was not low, nor was one step enough for the ascent of it, but it had a succession of many steps, and was of great height to climb. 8. And there were brought forward companies of confessors one by one, whom that 25 judge commanded to be put to death by the sword. And it came to my turn. 9. Then I heard a voice loud beyond all measure of one saying: "Make Marian come up." 10. And I was climbing that scaffold, when lo of a sudden there appeared to me sitting on that judge's right Cyprian, and 30 he stretched out his hand, and lifted me on to the higher part of the scaffold, and smiled, and said: " Come, sit with me." 11. And so it was that, while I still sat by his side, the other companies had audience. And that judge rose, and we escorted him to his palace. 12. Now our 35

road lay through a country lovely with meadows, and clad
with rich leafage of green woods, shady with cypresses
rising to the height and with pine-trees that knocked at
the door of heaven, so that you might think that place to
be crowned through the whole round of its circumference
with green groves. 13. The hollow in the midst abounded
with fertilizing rivulets flowing from a clear spring and
with pure waters. And behold of a sudden the judge
vanished from our eyes. 14. Then at this point Cyprian
caught up a bowl, which was lying by the edge of the
spring, and when he had filled it as one athirst from the
spring, he drained it, and filling it again handed it to me,
and I drank gladly. And as I said " Thanks be to God ",
awakened by the sound of my own voice I rose.'

VII. 1. Then it came back to the memory of James
also that a manifestation of the Divine favour had signified
this crown to him. 2. For during the preceding days when
Marian and James, and myself with them, were making
our journey together in the same carriage, about midday,
as we were travelling along those rough parts of the road
he was overtaken by a strange deep sleep. When, being
disturbed and roused by us, he awoke, ' I was troubled,'
he said, ' my brothers, not without joy; but you must
rejoice with me. 3. I beheld a youth of great height,
beyond telling, whose dress was a robe ungirt, that shone
with a light so dazzling that the eye could not look upon
it steadfastly: his feet did not tread the earth, and his
countenance was above the clouds. 4. As he ran past us,
he tossed into my lap two purple girdles, one for you,
Marian, and one for me, and said: " Follow me quickly." '
5. O sleep more active than all waking hours! O sleep
in which he slumbers happily who watches in faith!
Which had lulled only the earthy members, since none
but the spirit could see the Lord. 6. How exultant, how
lofty must the souls of those martyrs be believed to have

been, to whom, as about to suffer in the confession of His Sacred Name, it was given to hear and see Christ beforehand, offering Himself to His own in any place, at any time. 7. The restless jolting of the travelling carriage was no bar, nor the midday, then blazing in an unclouded sun. 5 8. He did not wait for the solitude of night: by a new kind of grace the Lord chose for His martyr a new time of vision.

VIII. 1. Nor was this favour shown to one only, or two. For there was a certain Aemilian, who, though he 10 was reckoned of equestrian rank among the heathen, was for all that in prison, and himself one of the brethren, who had lived from boyhood up to nearly his fiftieth year in celibacy. After fasts prolonged with double strictness in prison and prayers often repeated, through which his 15 devout soul found nourishment, and prepared for the Sacrament of the Lord on the morrow, he lay down in slumber at midday, and soon after, when sleep was flown, declared to us the secrets of his vision. 2. ' I was led from prison ', he told us, ' and a heathen, my brother in the 20 flesh, met me. 3. He, being very curious about our affairs, asked in an insulting voice how long we were going to remain in the penal darkness and starvation of the prison. 4. I gave him answer that the soldiers of Christ had in darkness most clear light, and in fasting the Word of God 25 for food most satisfying. 5. When he heard this, he said : " Be assured that for all you who are shut up in prison there remains, if you obstinately persist, the punishment of death." 6. But I, who feared that he might be playing with a lie made up to deceive me, wished to make my 30 desire a certainty, so I said to him: " Shall we indeed suffer all ? " 7. And he again declared: " Sword and blood are nigh at hand for you. But I would like to know," he went on, " whether for you who despise this present life the rewards bestowed in heaven are equal and unvarying 35

to each and all." 8. My answer was : " I am not capable
of giving decision on so great a matter. Lift ", I said,
" your eyes for a moment to heaven : you will see a count-
less multitude of flashing stars. Does every star shine
5 pre-eminent in equal glory of light ? And yet the light of
all is one." To this he replied with a still more searching
question : " If then there be some variety of reward, which
of you rank higher in earning the goodwill of your Lord ? "
" Two indeed above the rest," I answered, " whose names
10 must not be told to you, and are known to God." Finally,
when he pressed me more closely and became more
offensive in his questions, " They are those ", I said, " who
are crowned more gloriously, the tardier and more difficult
their victory; and for this it was written : " It is easier for
15 a camel to go through a needle's eye, than for a rich man
to enter into the kingdom of heaven." '

IX. 1. After these visions they remained a few days
more in prison, and were then brought into open court,
that the magistrates of Cirta might send them on, dis-
20 tinguished by the record of their brave confession, with
the account of the first stage in their condemnation to the
governor. 2. And behold one of our brethren standing
near drew the eyes of all the heathen to him, since already
in virtue of his coming passion Christ shone in his face
25 and look. 3. And when they demanded of him with
violence and fury whether he too were of the same religion
and Name, he snatched by quick confession at such sweet
companionship. 4. So the blessed martyrs, while preparing themselves for martyrdom, gained by reason of their
30 records more witnesses to God; and being now sent on
to the governor, hastened with goodwill on a troublesome
and difficult journey. 5. Then after an audience of the
governor they were guests again of the prison at Lambesa.
For this is the only hospitality provided by the heathen
35 for the just.

X. 1. Meanwhile, the bloodshed of many days was sending to the Lord numbers of our brotherhood, nor could the rage of the infuriate governor, busy in dealing so many blows at the laity, reach his victims Marian and James and the rest of the clergy. 2. For scheming cruelty 5 had carefully divided the different ranks of our religion, imagining that the laity separated from the clergy would yield to the temptations of the world and their own fears. 3. So my beloved and faithful soldiers of Christ and the rest of the clergy began to be a little downcast that the 10 laity should have completed the glory of their contest, while for themselves was reserved so sluggish and so late a victory.

XI. 1. Agapius, who had long ago completed his campaigns for the faith he had crowned by his martyrdom, had 15 been used to pray with supplications often repeated on behalf of two young women, Tertulla and Antonia, whom he loved as daughters very dearly, that they too might by the favour of God become martyrs with him, and had gained assurance of his merits by the following revelation. 20 2. For it was said to him : 'Why are you continually asking what you have merited by a single prayer?' 3. This Agapius appeared at that time to James while he was in prison during the time of sleep. For in the very moment of his passion, while he was awaiting the executioner, 25 'Good,' said James, ' I am on my way to the banquet of Agapius and the other blessed martyrs. 4. For last night, brothers, I saw our dear Agapius amid all the rest who were shut up along with us in the prison at Cirta exceeding glad, and holding a solemn and joyful banquet. 5. And 30 when I and Marian in the spirit of love and charity hurried thither as to a Love-feast, there ran up to meet us a boy, who was clearly one of the twins who had suffered three days before with their mother, with a garland of roses round his neck, bearing in his right-hand a bright green 35 palm-branch. 6. "Why are you in such haste?" he said, "Rejoice and be exceeding glad, for to-morrow you also will dine with us."'

7. O great and glorious favour of God to His own! O true and fatherly kindness of Jesus Christ our Lord, who grants to His beloved benefits so bountiful, and declares before bestowing the gifts of His mercy. 8. When the first day after the vision dawned, the sentence of the governor rendered homage to the promises of God, that sentence which restored at last Marian and James and the rest of the clergy to the patriarchs in glory, and delivered them from the miseries of this present world. 9. For they were led to the scene of their crown, a place sunk in the midst of a river-valley with lofty hills on either bank: the high ground on either side served also for seats as in a theatre. 10. In the middle of the hollow the river-channel itself drank the blood of the Blessed. Nor was there wanting both kinds of Sacrament, since they were not only baptized in their own blood but washed in the river.

XII. 1. You might have seen then strange and ingenious short cuts in savagery. For since the numbers of the just were a burden to the hand of the executioner, and to the sword itself which had so many necks to deal with, inventive cruelty arranged rows or lines drawn up in order, that the blade of the impious murderer might take the beheading of the faithful in a rush of fury. 2. And secondly he devised for himself this way of expediting his wickedness that the bloody and barbarous task might not prove beyond his powers. 3. For, if he had stood in one place to give the blow, the heaped-up bodies would have risen to a huge pile; and finally the channel of the river would have been choked by so great a heap of slaughter and have left no room.

4. When their eyes were bandaged according to custom

before the sword-stroke, no darkness shrouded the sight
of the free soul, but a rich inestimable blaze of light immeasurable shone upon them. 5. For many, with their
relatives and the brethren sitting by them, though their
eyes were not open for carnal vision, yet declared they saw 5
marvellous things, an appearance of horses in heaven white
as snow, on which rode young men clad in white. 6. And
there were not wanting some of the same company of
martyrs who confirmed by their ears the stories of their
comrades, and recognized their truth by the neighing and 10
noise of the horses which they heard. 7. There and then
Marian also, filled with the spirit of prophecy, con-
fidently and boldly foretold the quick avenging of the blood
of the righteous, and as though from the height of heaven
threatened diverse temporal plagues, pestilence, captivities, 15
famine, earthquakes, and the tormenting poisons of flies.
8. By this prophetic utterance the faith of the martyr not
only triumphed over the heathen but sounded in the ears
of the brethren a note, as it were a trumpet-blast, of a
courage for them to emulate, that amid so great temporal 20
plagues the saints of God might snatch the chance of a
death so good and precious.

XIII. 1. When all was over the mother of Marian,
exalting with a joy like that of the mother in the days of
the Maccabees, sure, his passion finished, of her son, began 25
to congratulate not him only but herself, who had borne
so great a child. 2. Her religious devotion embraced in the
body of her son the glory of her own womb, and imprinted
on the very wounds in his neck repeated kisses. 3. O Mary
rightly named! O mother blessed both in thy son and in 30
thy name! Who could believe that in her thus honoured in
the offspring of her womb the happy fortune of so great
a name ever went astray? 4. Truly inestimable is the
mercy of God Almighty and His Christ towards His own,
whom for their trust in His Name He not only strengthens 35

with the favour of His grace, but quickens with Redemption through His Blood! 5. For who can measure His benefits according to their proper worth? Who in this also works ever with a father's tenderness, that the very ransom which we believe to be paid in our own blood is provided by Almighty God: whose is the glory for ever and ever. Amen.

X

MARTYRDOM OF S. MARINUS (A. D. 262)

MARINUS was martyred in the reign of Gallienus in A. D. 262. But, as Gallienus had issued an edict of toleration in 261 (v. opening sentence), Marinus must have suffered from the unauthorized sentence of the governor Achaeus, or more probably by command of Macrianus, the instigator of the Valerian persecution, who had revolted from Gallienus and taken possession of Egypt, Palestine, and the East. He would naturally take the opportunity of venting his old hatred on the Christians whom his rival favoured. Eusebius goes on to tell us in the next chapter (*H.E.* vii. 16) that the body of Marinus was wrapt in a rich shroud and buried with all honours by a high-born senator of Rome, called Asterius. S. Marinus's festival is March 3.

Text from EUSEBIUS, *Hist. Eccl.* vii. 15

1. IN their time when there was peace everywhere in all the Churches, Marinus, being one of those who had distinguished himself in military service, a man eminent by birth and wealth, was beheaded at Caesarea in Palestine on account of his witness for Christ. The occasion was 5 as follows:

2. There is a honour among the Romans known as the ' vine-switch ', and they who obtain it are called ' centurions '. There being a place vacant his rank in the service entitled Marinus to this promotion. When he was on 10 the point of succeeding to the honour some one appeared before the tribunal, and alleged that it was not lawful for him according to ancient precedent to have any part in the dignities of Rome since he was a Christian and did not sacrifice to the Emperors; and that the position fell to himself. 15

3. The judge moved thereat (his name was Achaeus) first asked Marinus what his opinions were, and, when he saw that he resolutely confessed himself a Christian, gave him three hours' interval for consideration.

4. When he came outside the court, Theotecnus, the bishop of that district, went up to him in friendly fashion, and taking him by the hand led the way to the church, entered and placed him close to the very Altar. He then 5 drew back Marinus's cloak a little, and pointed to the sword as it hung at his side; at the same time he brought him the book of the Holy Gospels, and set it opposite, bidding him choose of the two that which was to his mind. When he without hesitation stretched out his right hand 10 and took the Divine Scriptures, 'Hold fast then,' said Theotecnus to him, 'Hold fast to God; and may you, strengthened by Him, obtain what you have chosen, go in peace.'

5. And immediately on his return from thence the voice 15 of the crier was heard in front of the court calling for him; for already the time allowed him was fulfilled. So he stood before the judge, and, after showing zeal beyond belief, was forthwith, as he was, led away to death and perfected.

XI

ACTS OF S. MARCELLUS (OCTOBER 30, A. D. 298)

MARCELLUS was martyred in the reign of Diocletian, A. D. 298, before the beginning of the Great Persecution in 303. There were, however, isolated cases of persecution before the latter date, especially in the army, Eusebius says, ' one or two here and there ' (*Hist. Eccl.* viii. 4). Another case was that of Maximilian (Ruinart, *Acta Mart.*, p. 340) in 295. These cases of soldier martyrs have a special interest. Some Christians, of whom the said Maximilian was one, especially those who, like Tertullian in his later days, belonged to the Montanist or Puritan sect, regarded all military service as unlawful. That this was not the general opinion among Christians is evidenced by the case of S. Marinus (p. 119) and of S. Marcellus here, and is otherwise abundantly clear. The story of the Thundering Legion proves it. The Christians would never have dared, or wished, to attribute supernatural intervention to the prayers of Christian soldiers (the general belief in something miraculous is evident from pagan and Christian writers alike), unless the army had been full of them. The adoption by Constantine of the Labarum as his standard in gratitude to the God of the Christians is to the same effect. And even Tertullian (*Apol.* xxxvii) says : ' We are men of yesterday ; yet we have filled all your places of resort— cities, islands, villages, free towns, market towns, *even the camp*, tribes, town-councils, palace, senate, forum ; we have left you nothing but your temples.'   *Text from* KNOPF

I. IN the city of Tingis, during the administration of Fortunatus as governor, the time came for the birthday of the Emperor. When all in that place were feasting at banquets and sacrificing, a certain Marcellus, one of the centurions of the Trajan legion, deeming those banquets to be heathen, cast away his soldier's belt in front of the 5 standards of the legion which were then in camp, and testified in a loud voice, saying : ' I serve Jesus Christ the

Eternal King.' He also threw away his vine-switch and arms, and added : 'Henceforward I cease to serve your Emperors, and I scorn to worship your gods of wood and stone, which are deaf and dumb idols. If such be the
5 terms of service that men are forced to offer sacrifice to gods and Emperors, behold I cast away my vine-switch and belt, I renounce the standards, and refuse to serve.'

II. The soldiers were dumbfounded at hearing such
10 things; they laid hold on him, and reported the matter to Anastasius Fortunatus the commander of the legion, who ordered him to be thrown into prison. When the feasting was over, he gave orders, sitting in council, that the centurion Marcellus should be brought in. When
15 Marcellus, one of the centurions of Asta, was brought in, Anastasius Fortunatus the governor said : 'What did you mean by ungirding yourself in violation of military discipline, and casting away your belt and vine-switch?'

Marcellus answered : 'On the 21st of July, in presence
20 of the standards of your legion, when you celebrated the festival of the Emperor, I made answer openly and in a loud voice that I was a Christian and that I could not serve under this allegiance, but only under the allegiance of Jesus Christ the son of God the Father Almighty.'

25 Anastasius Fortunatus the governor said : 'I cannot pass over your rash conduct, and therefore I will report this matter to the Emperors and Caesar. You yourself shall be referred unhurt to my lord, Aurelius Agricolan, Deputy for the Prefects of the Guard (the shorthand-
30 writer who took down the official proceedings was Caecilius).'

III. On the 30th of October at Tingis, Marcellus, one of the centurions of Asta, having been brought into court, it was officially reported : 'Fortunatus the governor has
35 referred Marcellus, a centurion, to your authority. There

is in court a letter dealing with his case, which at your command I will read.'

Agricolan said : ' Let it be read.'

The official report was as follows : ' From Fortunatus to you, my lord, and so forth. This soldier, having cast 5 away his soldier's belt, and having testified that he was a Christian, spoke in the presence of all the people many blasphemous things against the gods and against Caesar. We have therefore sent him on to you, that you may order such action to be taken as your Eminence may ordain 10 in regard to the same.'

IV. After the letter had been read, Agricolan said : ' Did you say these things as appear in the official report of the governor ? '

Marcellus answered : ' I did.'   15

Agricolan said : ' Did you hold the rank of a centurion of the first class ? '

Marcellus answered : ' I did.'

Agricolan said : ' What madness possessed you to cast away the signs of your allegiance, and to speak as you did ? ' 20

Marcellus answered : ' There is no madness in those who fear the Lord.'

Agricolan said : ' Did you make each of these speeches contained in the official report of the governor ? '

Marcellus answered : ' I did.'   25

Agricolan said : ' Did you cast away your arms ? '

Marcellus answered : ' I did. For it was not right for a Christian, who serves the Lord Christ, to serve the cares of the world.'

V. Agricolan said : ' The acts of Marcellus are such 30 as must be visited with disciplinary punishment.' And he pronounced sentence as follows : ' Marcellus, who held the rank of centurion of the first class, having admitted that he has degraded himself by openly throwing off his allegiance, and having besides put on record, as appears in 35 the official report of the governor, other insane expressions, it is our pleasure that he be put to death by the sword.'

When he was being led to execution, he said to Agricolan : ' May God bless thee ! For so ought a martyr to depart out of this world.'

And when he had said these words he was beheaded, dying for the name of our Lord Jesus Christ, Who is glorious for ever and ever. Amen.

XII

PASSION OF S. CASSIAN (December 3, a.d. 298)

This is a pendant to the Acts of S. Marcellus. S. Cassian is referred to in Prudentius, the famous Christian poet, Περὶ στεφάνων *Hymn.* iv. 45 : 'His city Tingis will repeat the name of Cassian.'

Text from Ruinart, *Acta Mart.*, p. 345

I. WHEN Aurelius Agricolan was acting as deputy for the Prefects of the Praetorian Guard, at the time when he was preparing to hear the case of the holy martyr Marcellus, the blessed Cassian was a shorthand-writer under the orders of his staff. So when Marcellus, one of 5 the centurions of Asta, was brought into court at Tingis on the 30th of October, Aurelius Agricolan by his power as judge strove with many threats to seduce him from perseverance in his confession. But the blessed Marcellus by the power of his constancy, so that all henceforward 10 considered him his judge's judge, proclaimed that he was the soldier of Christ, and could not serve the cares of the world, while Aurelius Agricolan on the other hand poured forth words full of fury. Cassian was taking down these statements, but, when he saw Aurelius Agrico- 15 lan, beaten by the devotion of so great a martyr, pronounce sentence of death, he vowed with an imprecation he would go no farther, and threw on the ground his pen and note-book. So, amid the astonishment of the staff and the laughter of Marcellus, Aurelius Agricolan trembling 20 leapt from the bench and demanded why he had thrown down his note-books with an oath. Blessed Cassian answered that Agricolan had dictated an unjust sentence. To avoid further contradiction, Agricolan ordered him to be at once removed and cast into prison. 25

II. Now the blessed martyr Marcellus had laughed

because, having knowledge of the future through the Holy Spirit, he rejoiced that Cassian would be his companion in martyrdom. On that very day amid the eager expectation of the city blessed Marcellus obtained his desire.
5 After no long interval, namely, on the 3rd of December, the worshipful Cassian was brought into the same court in which Marcellus had been tried, and by almost the same replies, the same statement as holy Marcellus had made merited to obtain the victory of martyrdom, through the
10 help of our Lord Jesus Christ, to Whom belong honour and glory, excellency and power for ever and ever. Amen.

XIII

PASSION OF S. PROCOPIUS (A. D. 303)

THE notice of the Martyrdom of S. Procopius, 'the great Martyr,' in Eusebius's *Martyrs of Palestine*, ch. i, runs as follows : ' Procopius therefore, the first of the Martyrs of Palestine, immediately on his first entrance before he made trial of imprisonment, being brought before the court of the Governor and bidden to sacrifice to the gods so-called, said that he knew one God alone to whom it was right he should be willing to sacrifice. And when he was bidden to offer libations to the four Emperors (Diocletian and Maximian, Augusti, Galerius and Constantius, Caesars) he uttered a sentence which pleased them but little, quoting a verse of the poet—" The rule of many lords is not good ; let there be One Lord, One King." On the 7th of the month Daesius (the 7th day before the Ides of June according to the Roman Calendar) on the 4th day of the week this, the first sign (i.e. martyrdom) at Caesarea in Palestine, was consummated.'

The account given in the text is from a fragment of the longer recension of the above work of Eusebius preserved in the Latin Passionaries, the only Latin fragment in existence of this recension.

The truth of this pure and simple story was overlaid by his later hagiographers with melodramatic absurdities and incredible marvels (see Gen. Introd., p. 13-4). S. Procopius suffered in the persecution of Diocletian, A. D. 303. His day both in the East and in the West is July 8.   *Text from* RUINART, *Acta Mart.*, p. 387

I. THE first of the martyrs in Palestine who has come to light was Procopius, a man filled with Divine grace, who so ordered his life before his martyrdom, that even from childhood he ever devoted himself to chastity and moral virtues. Indeed he so wore out his body, that to men's 5 thinking it was almost dead; but he so invigorated his spirit with the Word of God as by the refreshment of his spirit to minister strength to his body. His food and drink were bread and water : these were his only sustenance when after two or three days, sometimes even a week, he broke his fast. Moreover, meditation on the Divine Word had such a hold on his soul, that he continued therein night and day without being weary. An example of forbearance 5 and gentleness, while regarding himself as all men's inferior, he edified all men by his discourses. So great was his study in the Word of God. But of things without he had but little knowledge. By birth he belonged to Aelia, by abode or dwelling to Scythopolis. There he performed 10 three ecclesiastical functions : first, he held the office of Reader, secondly he interpreted in the Syrian tongue, thirdly he cast out devils by the imposition of hands.

II. When he had been taken with his companions from Scythopolis to Caesarea, he was led straight from the city 15 gates to the governor, and before making trial of distress of bonds or imprisonment at his very entrance he was urged by the judge Flavian to sacrifice to the gods. But he in a loud voice bare witness that there are not many gods but One, the Maker and Creator of all things. The 20 judge, being smitten by the stroke of his words and wounded in his conscience, agreed to what he said, and turned to other arguments, that at least he should sacrifice to the Emperors. But the holy martyr of God, despising his words, repeated a verse of Homer, saying : ' It is not 25 good there should be many lords. There is one Lord, one King.' And so, as soon as this speech of his was heard, he was led away to death by the command of the judge, as one who had uttered words of evil omen against the Emperors, and was beheaded. Thus the blessed one found 30 entrance into Heaven by the shortest way, on the 7th of the month of Desius, which among the Latins is called the Nones of July, in the first year of the persecution. This was the first martyrdom that was consummated at Caesarea, in the reign of our Lord Jesus Christ to whom 35 be honour and glory for ever and ever. Amen.

NOTES

I. MARTYRDOM OF S. POLYCARP

PAGE **32**, line 1. *dwells:* or 'dwelling as strangers and pilgrims', cf. Luke xxiv. 18, Acts vii. 6, Heb. xi. 9, 1 Pet. i. 17, id. ii. 11, Introd. to *1st Ep. of S. Clement*, Introd. *Ep. of Polycarp to the Philippians*.

l. 2. *Philomelium:* a town in Phrygia, in the centre of Asia Minor.

l. 4. *May the mercy, &c.* Jude 2.

l. 11. *conformable to the Gospel:* so Lightfoot, i. e. in accordance with the Gospel history of our Lord's Passion. He notices 'the tendency of these Acts to find parallels to our Lord's history in the final scenes of S. Polycarp's life', cf. chs. vi, vii, xvi.

l. 13. *looking, &c.:* Phil. ii. 4.

PAGE **33**, l. 4. *martyrdoms . . . God:* i. e. (v. end of ch. iv) those in which the sufferer does not provoke martyrdom, v. Matt. x. 23.

l. 14. *absent from the flesh:* cf. 2 Cor. v. 6, 8.

l. 15. *of their company:* cf. *Mart. Perp.*, ch. xv.

l. 23. *heart of man:* cf. 1 Cor. ii. 9, 1 Pet. i. 4.

l. 27. *harrows:* lit. *trumpeters* (κήρυκας), so from their resemblance to a trumpet, *shell-fish*, Lat. *murices*, so (from the prickles of the shell-fish) instruments of torture set with spikes, or, as Lightfoot thinks, the shells themselves which were used for purposes of torture, v. Ruinart, *Acta Mart.*, pp. 403, 408, 457.

l. 32. *Germanicus:* his day in the western Martyrologies is Jan. 19.

l. 34. *proconsul:* Lucius Statius Quadratus, a rhetorician and friend of the rhetorician Aristides.

PAGE **34**, l. 6. *Away, &c.:* Αἶρε, cf. Luke xxiii. 18, Acts xxi. 36.

l. 13. *who give themselves up:* reading τοὺς προδιδόντας ἑαυτούς.

l. 14. *teaching of the Gospel:* Matt. x. 23.

l. 21. *his custom:* v. Int., p. 32, and Polycarp, *Ep. to the Philippians*, ch. xii.

l. 30. *justice of the peace:* this officer's duty was to arrest disturbers of the peace (his name means lit. 'ruler of the peace'), and bring them before the judicial tribunals; he was a person chosen from among the leading men of the city and held office for a year. Lightfoot suggests 'High Sheriff' as the nearest equivalent.

l. 32. *Herod:* i. e. Herodes plays here a similar part to that of Herod Antipas in the death of Christ. The word κεκληρωμένος suggests (v. Lightfoot) that his name was not a mere chance but providential.

l. 33. *partner :* κοινωνός. Cf. Phil. iii. 10, 'The fellowship (κοινωνία) of His sufferings.'

l. 35. *constables :* diogmitae, light-armed police.

PAGE 35, l. 2. *Preparation :* the day before the Sabbath ; cf. Luke xxiii. 54, John xix. 31.

   against a thief : Matt. xxvi. 55.

l. 6. *will of the Lord :* Acts xxi. 14.

l. 10. *bade food and drink.* The Latin version, referring to Rom. xii. 20, Prov. xxv. 21, says : 'Not doing this without the command of the divine rule ; since it is written "Our enemies must be satisfied with drink and food"'.

l. 13. For *standing* in prayer v. Matt. vi. 5, Luke xviii. 11, 13.

l. 22. *High Sabbath :* σαββάτου μεγάλου. This in later times was the regular name for Holy Saturday, the day before Easter Sunday, but this use of the term seems to be two centuries later than Polycarp. Lightfoot takes it to mean any Sabbath which coincided with some great feast, possibly, in this case, the Feast of Purim, which, with its memories of the deliverance from massacre (Esther ix), would be likely to excite the Jews.

l. 26. *Caesar is Lord :* κύριος καῖσαρ : this, in this context, would be a direct negation of 'Jesus is Lord' (v. 1 Cor. xii. 3), and a deification of the Emperor.

PAGE 36, l. 2. *Be strong, &c. :* Josh. i. 6, 9, Deut. xxxi. 6, 23, 'Be strong and of a good courage', lit. 'play the man'. One MS. adds, 'For I am with thee (Acts xviii. 9, 10). For the voice from heaven cf. that to our Lord, John. xii, 28 and those to S. Peter, Acts. x. 13, 15, S. Paul, Acts ix. 4–7, xxii. 7, and S. Augustine at his conversion, "Tolle, Lege," "Take, Read," ' *Conf.* viii. 12.

l. 7. *the man :* adopting Lightfoot's reading.

l. 11. *Fortune of Caesar :* in Latin 'genius' or 'fortuna Caesaris.' The Christians were willing to swear 'per salutem' (*by the health* or *safety,*) of Caesar, but not by his genius or fortune, on the ground that these were demons, false gods (Tertullian, *Apol.* 32) (Lightfoot, note).

l. 17. *Swear, &c. :* this was the test applied by Pliny (*Ep.* x. 97, (96)) under Trajan (*c.* A.D. 112).

l. 18. *Eighty and six years :* this suggests, if it does not prove, that infant Baptism was, sometimes at least, practised even at this early date, A.D. 70 (156–86), the year of the fall of Jerusalem.

l. 27. *It is the people, &c. :* i. e. 'I would be willing to spare you, it is *the people* who are your enemies', cf. Pilate's attitude to our Lord. It is possible, however, as Lightfoot points out, that the proconsul knew the futility of the appeal, and wanted an excuse for his execution.

l. 29. *for we have been taught:* cf. Rom. xiii. 1, 7 ; 1 Pet. ii. 13–17. So S. Ignatius says (frag. 3) : 'Be obedient to Caesar in matters where obedience is without danger.' Ridley, *Conference with Latimer,* 1556, fo. 33, 'Policarpus, the moste constante Martyr, when he stode before the chiefe Ruler, and was commaunded to blaspheme Christ, and to sweare by the fortune of Caesar, &c. He aunswered with a milde spirite : We are taught (saieth he) to give honoure unto princes and those powers whiche be of God, but such honoure as is not contrarie to God's religion ' (Jacobson, *in loc.*).

l. 35. *For repentance, &c.:* i.e. ' It is you who should repent, not I.'

PAGE 37, l. 22. *Philip.* It is interesting (v. Lightfoot's note for particulars) that there are two inscriptions at Tralles giving the name of this Philip, and recording the fact that he had been Asiarch in A.D. 149 (seven years before S. Polycarp's martyrdom) and president of the games.

Asiarch : v. Acts xix. 31, ' The chief of Asia.' These ' Asiarchs ' were priestly officers, ten in number, elected by the various cities of the province of Asia, who celebrated at their own cost the public games and festivals (v. Page, *in loc.*), and were, therefore, men of wealth and position. Similar officers, Lyciarchae, Bithyniarchae, &c., existed elsewhere (Jacobson, *in loc.*).

l. 24. *wild beast combat.* The κυνηγέσια or *venatio* was a combat of wild beasts with another or with men, very popular among the Romans. There was one as early as 186 B.C., but they grew in magnificence till in the games celebrated by Trajan, after his victories over the Dacians, 11,000 animals were slaughtered. These were lions, bulls, elephants and rarer beasts, such as the rhinoceros and hippopotamus.

l. 27. *the vision :* v. ch. v.

PAGE 38. l. 1. *take off his shoes.* The early Christians used to take off the shoes of bishops and confessors. So in the account of the martyrdom of the Bishop Fructuosus we are told that Augustalis, his Reader, asked leave with tears to take off the martyr's shoes, ch. iii, p. 102.

l. 3. *even before his martyrdom :* or πρὸ τῆς πολιᾶς, 'even before his grey hairs came.'

l. 4. *goodness of his life.* The verb (πολιτεύομαι), connected with the substantive (πολιτεία) used here, is found in Phil. i. 27 (*Let your conversation be* as it becometh the gospel of Christ), and in Acts xxiii. 1, ' I have lived in all good conscience.'

l. 5. *things devised for his burning :* lit. ' The instruments (ὄργανα) fitted for the stake (pyre).' Some understand by this the shirt dipped in pitch, ' tunica molesta,' worn by the victims of the Neronian persecution, v. Juv. viii. 235, and Schol. It seems unlikely, however, that the writer, whose description is so minute, should have omitted to mention this by name. It might mean the chains to bind the hands and feet, v. next note.

l. 8. *For he that enabled me, &c.* Similar words were used by the martyr Theodorus (Vincent *specul. Historiale,* xii. 92). The nails were attached to the chains by which the sufferer was bound, not driven through the hands and feet, as in crucifixion, as is clear from S. Polycarp's words and from the ready agreement of the executioners.

l. 14. *burnt-offering.* The same Greek word ὁλοκαύτωμα occurs in the same sense in Lev. xvi. 24.

l. 20. *day and hour :* not of a literal day and hour ; the day is the period of suffering, the hour its climax (Lightfoot) ; cf. John xii. 27.

l. 22. *the cup :* cf. the request of the sons of Zebedee, Matt. xx. 22–3, and the Agony, *id.* xxvi. 39.

resurrection of life : S. John v. 29.

l. 27. *glorify Thee :* cf. the *Gloria in Excelsis.*

l. 31. *offered up the Amen.* The Greek word (ἀναπέμπω) is specially used of an offering of praise and thanksgiving, e. g. Clem. Al. *Paed.* iii. 12, 101–3, Just. Mart. *Apol.* i. 65 in a description of the Eucharist, ' Taking bread and a chalice of wine mingled with water he makes an offering of praise and glory to the Father of All through the Name of the Son and of the Holy Spirit.' The Great Amen was that said by all at the end of the Consecration Prayer, cf. *Mart. Perp.,* p. 81, l. 13 and note, and it is this Amen which is probably referred to here, as the culmination of S. Polycarp's *offering* of himself.

PAGE 39, l. 4. *burning in a furnace :* Rev. i. 15, of ' The Son of Man,' ' His feet like unto fine brass, as if they burned in a furnace.'

l. 9. *slaughterer :* Lat. *confector,* whose business it was to give the *coup de grâce* to a beast in the arena, or, as here and in the Acts of S. Perpetua, ch. xxi, p. 92, to a human being.

l. 10. *a dove and.* These words are almost certainly a later addition, and certainly not genuine in their present form. They are not found in Eusebius nor in the early Latin translation by Rufinus, nor even in the late historian Nicephorus, who was much addicted to the marvellous, and are absent from several of the Greek manuscripts here. Some suppose περιστερά, *dove,* to be a corruption of an earlier reading, perhaps ἐπ᾽ ἀριστερᾷ, on the *left,* or περὶ στύρακα 'about the sword-haft' (Wordsworth), others that there has crept into the text a reader's gloss, who noted ' The soul of P. at this moment fled to heaven ', the departing soul being frequently represented in early Christian art and literature under the form of a dove, e. g. Prudentius *Peristeph*. iii. 161 foll. : ' Then suddenly sprang forth a dove whiter than snow, that seemed to leave the mouth of the martyr and soar to heaven. This was the soul of Eulalia, milk-white, swift, and innocent.' Lightfoot regards them as a deliberate forgery by Pionius, v. note on p. 41, l. 21.

l. 27. Alce was a Christian ; she is saluted by S. Ignatius, both in his letter to the people of Smyrna, ch. xiii, and in his letter to S. Polycarp, ch. viii, as ' a name much longed for ', ποθητόν μου ὄνομα, perhaps with a play on the word. It was a divided household.

l. 29. *begin to worship him*. The same fears were expressed by the enemies of the Christians in the Diocletian persecution, v. Eus., *Hist. Eccl*. viii. 6 ; see also the *Acts of S. Fructuosus*, ch. ii, p. 101.

l. 34. *the sinless for sinners :* cf. 1 Pet. iii. 18, ' For Christ also hath once suffered for sins, the just for the unjust.'

PAGE 40, l. 10. *a convenient place*. The omission to describe the place is an interesting proof that the account is by a contemporary. It was feared that the heathen might remove or insult the relics.

l. 12. *birthday*. It was the custom to celebrate the day on which martyrs died, in place of the day on which they were born, as their ' heavenly birthday ', cf. an ancient commentator on Job : ' We do not celebrate the day of their birth, since that is the entrance into sorrows and all temptations ; but we celebrate the day of their death, as the release from all sorrows, and the banishment of all temptations : we celebrate the day of their death, because those do not die who seem to die.'

l. 32. *Marcion :* he was evidently the composer of the letter ; Euarestus was the scribe.

PAGE 41, l. 7. Xanthicus is the sixth month in the Ephesian calendar. The second of Xanthicus is Feb. 23rd, the traditional date throughout the East for S. Polycarp's Martyrdom. In the Latin calendar the festival is kept on Jan. 26. Feb. 23rd is no doubt the right date. The year was A. D. 155 (Lightfoot) or A. D. 156 (Turner). The Emperor was Antoninus Pius.

l. 8. *High Sabbath :* v. ch. viii and note.

l. 9. The eighth hour may mean either 8 a.m. reckoned from midnight, or 2 p.m. reckoned from 6 a.m. ; the former is the more probable, as these spectacles usually took place before midday.

l. 10. *chief priest* here means the same as Asiarch, above, ch. xii. Tralles, on a tributary of the Maeander, about thirty miles east of Ephesus, supplied, owing to the wealth of its inhabitants, a large proportion of the Asiarchs, v. note, ch. xii.

l. 20. This is Gaius the Presbyter, mentioned by Eusebius, Jerome, and Photius, now identified with Hippolytus, for a time an anti-Pope in the papacy of Callixtus, afterwards reconciled and martyred. His most famous work is the *Confutation of all Heresies*.

l. 21. S. Irenaeus was born at Smyrna *c.* A.D. 135-40, the city of which S. Polycarp became bishop. He was made Bishop of Lyons in A.D. 177 or 178 (cf. pp. 53-4), and died in 202 or 203. Two books of his survive: the treatise *Against Heresies*, which deals chiefly with the Gnostics and the Marcionites, and the *Demonstration of the Apostolic Teaching* ; cf. Int. to *Letter of Churches of Vienne and Lyons*. Lightfoot believes the whole of §§ (paragraphs) 2 and 3 to be an invention of the pseudo-Pionius there mentioned, who is the author of a 'Life of S. Polycarp ', full of legendary matter, and, so far as it can be tested, a pure fabrication. This Pionius would be the editor of this ' Martyrdom of Polycarp '. We have, however, almost the whole of it quoted or paraphrased in Eusebius, *Eccl. Hist.* iv. 15. Pionius seems to have inserted the mention of the dove in ch. xvi (v. Lightfoot, *Apost. Fathers*, pt. ii, vol. i, p. 644).

l. 27. *as I shall show.* The passage in which this promise is redeemed is not extant.

II. ACTS OF SS. CARPUS, PAPYLUS, AND AGATHONICA

PAGE 42, l. 1. *Pergamus :* the chief city of the province of Asia.

ll. 6, 12. *name is Christian: I am a Christian:* cf. *Letter of Churches of Vienne and Lyons*, ch. 20, where Sanctus answers to all questions, ' I am a Christian,' and confesses this instead of name and city and race and everything.

PAGE 43, l. 2. *counterfeit presentments.* S. Carpus's view of the heathen gods is that they are ' counterfeit (κιβδήλοις, properly used of coins) presentments of demons '. They have no existence (v. §§ 15, 16) ; there are no such beings as Jupiter, Apollo and the rest. But the demons or evil spirits are real, and these, working under the names of the gods, deceive men, having been themselves corrupted and incited to wickedness by the Devil, the Great Deceiver. So S. Augustine, *City of God*, ii. 4, speaks of ' unclean spirits that thus illude men under the names of Gods '.

l. 5. *in spirit and in truth :* John iv. 23.

l. 7. *eternal life through the Word :* cf. John i. 4, iii. 15, &c.

l. 9. *vanity :* ματαιότης. This and the adj. μάταιος are specially used of idols as *vain, unreal, useless* ; v. Acts xiv. 15, ' We . . . preach unto you that ye should turn from these vanities unto the living God.' Cf. Jer. ii. 5, Lev. xvii. 7, &c.

l. 13. *thereto :* i.e. to wickedness, or, more probably, to the deception of man. The words ' the demons ' are not found in the text. If they are omitted the object must be ' men ' ; but the Greek word for *provoked* παραζηλώσαντος is more naturally used of provoking other spirits to emulation than of tempting humanity, his dupes, cf. the use of the same word in Rom. x. 19, and xi. 11.

The beginning of this sentence is translated by Mason ' For just vengeance is taken of him, &c.' but it is very difficult to render μετά here as anything but ' with ' (δίκη ... δικαία ἐστὶν μετὰ τοῦ πλανήσαντος), and so Harnack, who suggests that one reason why S. Carpus speaks so much of the Devil is that he is a native of Pergamus, ' where Satan's seat is '. (Rev. ii. 13.)

l. 17. *Perish the gods, &c.* : Jer. x. 11.

l. 29. *know they are nothing* : v. note on p. 43, l. 2.

PAGE 44, l. 3. *fatherly love* : στοργή a beautiful word, specially used of *parental* love. It is never used in the New Testament, where the usual word for *love,* whether of God or man, is ἀγάπη. I have taken my translation of it from Mason.

l. 7. *by his experience* : ἀποπειράσας. So Mason translates it. Till I looked at him, I had translated it ' making conjecture of the things that shall happen ', and I think this is possible, and more in accordance with the ordinary usage of the word, but not so good here. Harnack agrees with Mason.

l. 9. *For by the decree of God, &c.* : ἔχει γὰρ ἐκ τῆς ἀποφάσεως τοῦ θεόν τὴν ἀδικίαν, ⟨καὶ⟩ τὸ εἰδέναι : καὶ is not in the text, there are two words with the same form ἀπόφασις (1) meaning *denial,* (2) a *judicial sentence.* Mason translating the text (without the καὶ) renders ' By his denial of God he has gained a knowledge of unrighteousness '. But τὴν ἀδικίαν τὸ εἰδέναι seems a very odd order, and the sense is not what is wanted here : whereas it is to the point to urge that the Devil, though fallen, retains his angelic intelligence, and so Harnack.

l. 12. *Consular* : ὑπατικέ, a man who has held the office of consul.

l. 19. *hung up and scraped.* This torture is described in the Life of S. Pamphilus by Eusebius, ch. v, ' scraping of the sides, and rubbing of the scraped parts with rough cloths of goat's wool ' : cf also Tert. *Apol.* xii, *Passio S. Bonifacii,* § 9, and Le Blant, *Actes des Martyrs,* p. 166, where a number of other examples are given.

l. 24. *councillor* : i.e. a member of the town-council, a ' decurio '.

l. 27. *Thyatira* : one of the Seven Cities of the Book of Revelation, in the Province of Asia, some 40 or 50 miles due N. of Sardis.

l. 32. *after his faith* : cf. 1 Cor. iv. 15, ' In Christ Jesus I have begotten you through the Gospel ' ; Tit. i. 4, ' To Titus, mine own son after the common faith ' ; cf. Philemon 10, 1 Pet. v. 13. Duchesne, however (*Early Hist. of the Church,* Eng. Trans., p. 193 note), compares Matt. xii. 48–50 ; in that case S. Papylus will mean Christians generally, not his own disciples. But the word ' children ', in conjunction with the other passages, shows, I think, that he refers to disciples, cf. note on p. 66, l. 13.

PAGE 45, l. 13. *the Enemy :* Satan, which has the same meaning in Hebrew.

l. 17. *nailed to the stake.* The nails were not driven through the hands and feet, as in crucifixion, but attached to chains or ropes by which the sufferer was bound to the stake; cf. *Martyrdom of S. Polycarp*, xiii, and note there.

PAGE 46, l. 1. *dinner hath been prepared :* Matt. xxii. 4 (cf. Luke xiv. 15).

ll. 6 ff. *Martyrdom of Agathonica.* Duchesne (v. note on p. 44, l. 32) points out, and Mason agrees, that the account here is incomplete. 'From the only manuscript remaining, the martyrdom of S. Agathonica would appear to have been in reality suicide ; nevertheless, the spectators exclaim : " Sad judgements ! Unjust orders ! " Clearly S. Agathonica had been condemned like the other two, and part of the text is here missing.' The Christians disapproved of those who courted martyrdom, v. *Martyrdom of S. Polycarp*, iv, and note on p. 33, l 4.

l. 7. *Protector :* προνοητής, ' He who provides '.

l. 8. *am come . . . .* I know three examples of this rare construction, which I regard as elliptical—(1) this passage ἐφ' ὃ πάρειμι, (*Let me do that) for which I am come ;* (2) Matt. xxvi. 50 ἐφ' ὃ πάρει (*Do that) for which thou art come* (R.V. etc.) ; (3) an inscription of the first century on a beaker (kindly communicated by a reader), εὐφραίνου ἐφ' ὃ πάρει. *Enjoy yourself.* (*Do that) for which you are here.* Others translate all three passages as questions—(1) *Wherefore am I here ?* (Harnack) ; (2) *Wherefore art thou come ?* (A.V., one Syr. vers., Harnack) ; (3) *What are you here for ?* The objection, in my opinion fatal, to this view is that the relative ὅς is never used in Greek (except possibly illiterate Greek) as an interrogative (v. Lobeck *Phryn.*, p. 57, Moulton *Gr. of N. T. Greek*, p. 93).

l. 13. *Lord, Lord, &c. :* Ps. cxliii. 9 ' Deliver me, O Lord, from mine enemies : for I flee unto Thee to hide me.'

l. 14. *perfected :* v. note on p. 69, l. 26.

III. ACTS OF SS. JUSTIN AND HIS COMPANIONS

PAGE 48, l. 4. *prefect.* The office of Prefect of the City (*praefectus urbi*) was first instituted by Augustus. He had all the powers necessary to maintain peace and order in Rome. There was no appeal from his sentence except to the Emperor himself. It was often the crowning-point of a political career.

l. 5. *Rusticus :* Q. Junius Rusticus, one of the teachers of the

Emperor M. Aurelius, a distinguished Stoic philosopher, and grandson of the friend of the famous Stoic Thrasea. He was much honoured, and often consulted on public as well as private matters by the emperor.

l. 8. *make submission to the Princes.* One of these was Marcus Aurelius Antoninus (v. p. 54), the famous Stoic philosopher, author of *The Meditations,* a man otherwise of exemplary life, but a great persecutor of the Christians. The martyrdoms of SS. Carpus, Papylus, and Agathonica (p. 42), the Scillitan martyrs (p. 71), the martyrs of Vienne and Lyons (p. 53), as well as those of SS. Justin and his companions all occurred in his reign. He associated with himself in the Empire his son-in-law, Lucius Verus.

PAGE 49, l. 4. *acquainted with all doctrines :* Justin was a philosopher ; v. Int., p. 47, and ch. v.

l. 19. *disciples :* Otto suggests, for μαθητῶν, μαθημάτων doctrines.

l. 26. *Where do ye meet together?* Possibly (v. Otto's note) Crescens, S. Justin's enemy (v. Int., p. 47), had accused him of forming a secret society, of which the Roman Government was always afraid.

PAGE 50, l. 1. *the baths of Timothy.* These were on the Viminal, so called because built by two brothers, Timothy and Novatus, said to be brothers of the martyrs SS. Pudentiana and Praxedis, commemorated in the ancient church of S. Pudentiana. The exact translation is very doubtful, perhaps, as Otto suggests, the name of Martin has been introduced by mistake.

l. 25. *Paeon stood up and said.* Paeon was not one of the accused, but made a voluntary confession.

PAGE 51, l. 2. *dragged away :* perhaps as a slave.

Iconium : the capital of Lycaonia, but originally part of Greater Phrygia, visited by S. Paul, Acts xiii. 51, xiv. xvi. 2.

l. 10. *acquainted with true doctrine.* The prefect is alluding to S. Justin's reputation as a philosopher, and particularly to his claim in ch. ii ; cf. Int., p. 47.

l. 14. *gifts :* δόματα. Cf. Eph. iv. 8, Ps. lxviii. 18, ' When He ascended up on high, He led captivity captive, and gave gifts unto men.'

l. 15. *consummation of the whole world :* Otto points out that the Christians still expected the end of the world to be near, cf. Justin, *Dial. Tryph.,* ch. xxviii.

free gift : χάρισμα a *free* gift of God, unearned, opposed in Rom. vi. 23 to ὀψώνια, what men have earned, ' For the wages of sin is death ; but the *gift* of God is eternal life through Jesus Christ our Lord ' ; cf. ibid. v. 15, 16 ' But not as the offence, so also is the *free gift* . . . The *free gift* is of many offences unto justification.'

l. 18. *fully persuaded :* πεπληροφόρημαι the same word as in Rom. iv. 21 (of Abraham) 'Being fully persuaded that what He had promised He was able also to perform ', a very strong expression ; cf. ibid. xiv. 5.

l. 29. *confidence :* παρρησία, confidence, boldness, frequent in the New Testament, e. g. 1 John iv. 17, ' That we may have boldness in the day of judgement ' ; cf. ibid. ii. 28, iii. 21, v. 14, 1 Tim. iii. 13, Heb. iii. 6, iv. 16, x. 19, 35, Eph. iii. 12.

l. 30. *judge the whole world :* cf. 2 Cor. v. 10, ' For we must all appear before the judgement-seat of Christ.'

IV. LETTER OF CHURCHES OF VIENNE AND LYONS

PAGE 57, l. 1. *the Adversary :* i. e. Satan.

l. 5. *from houses :* probably 'private houses ' of friends, tradesmen, &c. ; some, however, think it refers to ' public buildings '.

l. 7. *But the grace of God, &c.* This passage is full of reminiscences of the New Testament. For ' steadfast ' cf. 1 Cor. xv. 58 ' Wherefore, my beloved brethren, be ye stedfast ' ; Col. i. 23, ' If ye continue in the faith grounded and stedfast ' (A.V. ' settled '). For ' pillars ' cf. Rev. iii. 12, ' Him that overcometh will I make a pillar in the temple of my God ' ; also Gal. ii. 9, 1 Tim. iii. 15. For ' reproach ' Heb. x. 33.

l. 13. *the sufferings, &c. :* Rom. viii. 18.

l. 18. *beleaguerings :* As Routh points out, this word (συγκλείσεις) cannot here mean ' imprisonments ', which are not inflicted by the multitude, but prevention of the Christians from leaving their houses, or visiting other people, §. 5.

l. 21. *tribune :* a superior officer, of something the same rank as our colonel ; he has nothing to do with the ' Tribune of the Plebs '.

l. 22. *examined :* a technical word for the preliminary judicial inquiry.

l. 23. *governor :* of the ' provincia Lugdunensis,' an Imperial Legate.

l. 26. *Vettius Epagathus :* it appears both from the account here (v. § 10 *inf.*) and from the testimony of S. Gregory of Tours (6th cent.) *Hist. Franc.* i. 27 and 29 that he was a man of noble birth.

l. 30. *walked in all the commandments :* Luke i. 6.

l. 32. *great zeal for God :* Rom. x. 2.

l. 33. *fervent in spirit :* Rom. xii. 11 ; Acts xviii. 25.

PAGE 58, l. 2. *godless or impious.* As Mason points out, the words are used in their strict sense, though they would not worship the Roman gods, they were not ' godless ', nor ' impious ', though they would not offer incense to the emperor.

l. 7. *styled the advocate of the Christians :* according to the Latin he was so called by the judge, 'Advocatus quidem Christianorum iudicis elogio appellatus.'

l. 9. *the Spirit of Zacharias :* an allusion to Luke i. 67 : 'And his father Zacharias was filled with the Holy Ghost.' The Holy Spirit is called Παράκλητος, the Paraclete, translated 'Comforter', i. e. 'Strengthener', in the A.V., in John xiv. 16, 26 ; xv. 26 ; xvi. 7. The R. V. follows the A. V. giving in the margin 'Advocate' or 'Helper'. It is applied to the Son in 1 John ii. 1, where both A. V. and R. V. translate it 'Advocate', the R. V. giving 'Comforter', or 'Helper' in the margin. The Greek word means 'one called to the side of another', and so in the Classical writers an 'advocate', especially for the defence, in a court of law. The Greek Fathers, as a rule take it to mean 'consoler', 'comforter'. But Westcott on John xiv. 16 concludes that the passive form and the classical and New Testament use of the word are decisive for the passive sense 'Advocate'. Its unequivocal use here in so early a document as 'Advocate' is very interesting.

l. 11. *lay down his life :* 1 John iii. 16 ; John xv. 13.

l. 12. *a true disciple of Christ :* Luke xiv. 26–7 'If any man . . . hate not . . .his own life also, he cannot be My disciple.'

Following the lamb, &c. : Rev. xiv. 4.

l. 14. *were divided :* (διεκρίνοντο) prob., v. Routh, an athletic metaphor, referring to the examination of candidates for the games, after which some were accepted, and some rejected.

were protomartyrs : i. e. the first martyrs in the Churches of Lyons and Vienne, perhaps in Gaul. There is conjectured to have been a Christian colony at Marseilles in the 2nd century, otherwise this is the first mention of Christianity in Gaul.

l. 16. *confession :* they had made their confession already (§ 8).

l. 19. *miscarried.* The substantive (ἔκτρωμα) connected with the verb used here (ἐκτιτρώσκω) is used in the Old Testament for men in great misery (Job. iii. 16 ; Eccles. vi. 3), and once in the New Testament by S. Paul of himself (1 Cor. xv. 8) 'And last of all He was seen of me also, as of one born out of due time.' It is naturally used here of apostates : Christ had said to Nicodemus (John iii. 7) 'Ye must be born again ' ; these had indeed, as members (probably baptized) of the Christian community, been 'born again', but they had been born dead, or, at best, mis-shapen and incomplete ; cf. §§ 45–6.

l. 29. *two Churches.* of Lyons and Vienne.

l. 35. *Thyestean banquets.* Atreus killed the two sons of his brother Thyestes and served up their flesh before their father at a banquet. The curse on the house of Tantalus, of which Atreus was a member, was a favourite subject of Greek tragedy. The charge of ‘Thyestean banquets’ was commonly urged against the Christians, and is found in the famous letter of Pliny, in the very beginning of the 2nd century. Oedipus unwittingly killed his own father and married his own mother.

These stories of cannibalism and incest are alluded to by Justin, *Apol.* i. 26 ; Eusebius, *H. E.* iv. 7 ; Irenaeus, *Haer.* i. 25. 3, and others. They suggest that they are due to the conduct of heretics, especially of the followers of Carpocrates, an early Gnostic, who held that ‘works were indifferent, and were good and bad in human opinion only. His followers . . . completely reversed the notions of good and evil’ (Foakes-Jackson, *History of the Christian Church*, p. 136). The Holy Communion misinterpreted may have given occasion for charges of cannibalism ; and Oecumenius (? 10th cent.) on 1 Pet. p. 498 maintains that these slaves, who, as heathen, had never seen it celebrated, did so misinterpret what they had overheard their masters say.

PAGE 59, l. 6. *friendship :* the Greek word οἰκειότης covers both friendship and kinship.

l. 7. *gnashed their teeth :* the same Greek word διεπρίοντο, which literally means ‘to cut through with a saw’, and so, from the saw-like motion, ‘to gnash the teeth’, is found in Acts vii. 54, and v. 33, where it is translated ‘they were cut to the heart’, but in view of the context the more literal version seems better here.

‘*whosoever killeth you*’, &c. : John xvi. 2.

l. 16. Pergamus, one of the Seven Churches of the Apocalypse, was a Greek city in Asia Minor. Asia Minor during the second century was ‘the great seed-bed of Christianity’ (Mason). ‘The Christian churches of Gaul, in particular, were very closely bound to those of Asia Minor’ (ibid.). Marseilles was founded in 600 B.C. by Phocaea, a city of Asia Minor. ‘Greek commerce had spread up the valley of the Rhone, and the towns of Vienne and Lyons . . . were largely Greek-speaking towns.’

l. 17. *pillar and stay :* 1 Tim. iii. 15, where these words are used of the Church at Ephesus. They are used of a person in Greg. Naz. *Ep.* 44 (29), ‘What am I to call you ? στύλον καὶ ἑδραίωμα τῆς Ἐκκλησίας.’

l. 24. *according to the flesh :* cf. Eph. vi. 5, ‘Servants, be obedient to them that are your masters according to the flesh’, cf. Col. iii. 22.

PAGE 60, l. 9. *range himself :* it is a military word : Sanctus is one of the army of ‘steadfast pillars’ spoken of in § 6, where the same Greek word is used.

l. 22. *issuing from the belly.* The reference is to John vii. 38,

' He that believeth on Me, as the Scripture hath said, out of his belly shall flow rivers of living water.' The original of the image is the Rock in Horeb (Exod. xvii. 6 ; Num. xx. 11 ; cf. 1 Cor. x. 4, ' They drank of that spiritual Rock that followed them : and that Rock was Christ '). Westcott (*in loc.*) refers also to Isa. lviii. 11 ; Zech. xiv. 8. Our author is bringing out the implications of the passage in S. John : the believer ' becomes in his turn a rock from within which the waters flow to slake the thirst of others ', but those waters are derived from the original Spiritual Rock, which is Christ.

l. 24. *bent double :* συνεσπασμένον, it may mean ' wrenched ', but that, as Routh points out, would rather be διεσπασμένον.

l. 27. *a pattern :* cf. 1 Tim. i. 16, ' That in me first Jesus Christ might show forth all long-suffering, for a pattern to them which should hereafter believe on Him to life everlasting.'

l. 31. *his body :* plur. in the Gk., τῶν σωμάτων, v. Rob. for similar examples.

PAGE 61, l. 7. *devoured :* in allusion to 1 Pet. v. 8, ' The Devil, as a roaring lion, walketh about, seeking whom he may devour ', where the same Greek word is used.

l. 12. The *slumber* is, of course, the sleep of sin, cf. Rom. xiii. 11 ; 1 Cor. xv. 34 ; 1 Thess. v. 6, 7, which is compared here and in the passages from 1 Cor. and 1 Thess. to the sleep of drunkenness.

l. 15. *How can those eat, &c. ?* This is interesting showing that the law passed at the Council of Jerusalem (Acts xv. 29) ' That ye abstain from . . . blood ' was still observed nearly 130 years after. So Tertullian (2nd cent.) *Apol.* 9 says that Christians abstained ' from blood and from things strangled ', cf. Clement of Alexandria (2nd cent.) *Paed.* iii. 3 near the end. In the Eastern Church the observance remains to this day : in the Western it is said to have lasted till the 12th century, but in Africa, at all events, it had passed away by the time of S. Augustine who laughs at such scruples (*c. Faustum Manich.* 32. 13). The question whether the law was still applicable was discussed in England in the 18th century, and again by Dr. Pusey (Tertullian, *Lib. of Fathers*, p. 107).

l. 23 *stocks :* the Greek word ξύλον is the same as the Latin *nervus*. It was a log of wood with five holes at either end.

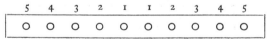

The feet of the prisoner were inserted in these and stretched. Insertion in the fifth holes involved the maximum amount of strain, cf. *Acts of SS. Perp. et Felic.* viii, p. 83).

PAGE **62**, l. 1. Pothinus (his name is Greek, Ποθεινός '*Desired*')
was Bishop of Lyons, probably at this time the only Bishop in Gaul,
Vienne being administered by a deacon (Sanctus).   He was no doubt
an Asiatic Greek (v. 59, l. 16, note), and very possibly, like his successor
S. Irenaeus, a disciple of S. Polycarp, who was himself a disciple of
S. John (v. p. 31).

l. 8. *Christ might triumph :* cf. 2 Cor. ii. 14.

l. 12. *a good confession :* cf. 1 Tim. vi. 13, ' Christ Jesus, who before
Pontius Pilate witnessed a good confession.'   The Greek here means
lit. ' gave good witness ', but, as the allusion to 1 Tim. is clear, it
seemed to me best to give the words, only slightly different, of S. Paul.

l. 25. *mercy of Christ.*   What is ' the immeasurable mercy of Christ'
which is here spoken of ?   Clearly the recovery of most of the lapsed,
as is shown by the repetition of the same phrase in § 45.

PAGE **63**, l. 2. *Spirit of the Father.*   The Holy Spirit proceeds,
according to the Western Church, from the Father and the Son,
according to the Eastern from the Father only.   The doctrine,
however, of the Procession was not yet defined at this date (A. D. 177).

l. 7. *as for a bride, &c.*   This refers to the Septuagint version of
Ps. xlv. 14 (slightly altered).   Our Prayer Book version has, ' She
shall be brought unto the King in raiment of needlework.'

l. 9. *savour of Christ :* cf. 2 Cor. ii. 15, ' We are unto God a sweet
savour of Christ.'   Compare the burning of S. Polycarp (*Mart. S. Polyc.*
xv, p. 39), when the bystanders smelt ' a sweet scent as of frankincense
or other precious spice '.

l. 28. *special day :* i. e. a special day beyond the days regularly
assigned to the fights with beasts.   Leave for such a day was difficult to
obtain : it was refused in the case of S. Polycarp (*Mart. S. Polyc.* ii, p. 37).

l. 33. *bouts.*   The Greek word used here, κλῆρος, is a technical word
for a ' heat '.   The martyrs had, as it were, won the preliminary heats,
and had now secured their place in the final.

l. 35. *gauntlet of whips :* cf. *Pass SS. Perp. and Felic.* xviii, and note
there.

PAGE **64**, l. 7. *Sanctus :* v. § 20.

l. 13. Blandina, as a slave, was crucified.

l. 25. *crooked Serpent :* Isa. xxvii. 1.

l. 27. *put on Christ :* Rom. xiii. 14, ' But put ye on the Lord Jesus
Christ ' ; cf. Gal. iii. 27.

l. 28. *bouts :* See above, p. 63, l. 33, note.

PAGE **65**, l. 5. *dispatch to Caesar.*   So S. Paul's case, because he
was a Roman citizen, is referred to Caesar, Acts xxv. 10–12.

l. 7. *not idle nor unfruitful :* cf. 2 Pet. i. 8, ' They made you that ye
shall be neither barren (marg. *idle*) nor unfruitful.'   The reference is

very interesting, because there are very few early references to 2 Peter, and its authenticity was questioned even in the Early Church. There is another clear reference to it in § 48 ; v. note, p. 66, l. 3.

l. 12. *Virgin Mother :* a beautiful name for the Church, which is spoken of as ' Mother ' below, ii. 6 and 7.

l. 13. *untimely births :* cf. p. 58, l. 19, and note.

l. 15. *entered again into their mother's womb :* taking the reading of the cod. Reg., adapted by Routh and Migne, ἀνεμητροῦντο (from μήτρα, *womb*), a word nowhere else found, but exactly suitable to the context, they were received again into the womb of their Mother, the Church. The ordinary reading ἀνεμέτρουντο must mean *were remade*, but this involves an unnatural extension of the word's usual meaning, *to remeasure, trace back again*, in which it is actually employed in § 55.

l. 18. *death of the wicked :* Ezek. xxxiii. 11, cf. ibid. xviii. 32.

l. 19. *made sweet their bitterness :* lit. ' making them sweet within ' ; the *sweetness* of repentance contrasted with the *bitterness* of sin. Sin is spoken of as *bitterness* (πικρία) in Acts viii. 23, ' I perceive that thou art in the gall of bitterness, and in the bond of iniquity ', and Heb. xii. 15 (cf. Deut. xxix. 18) ' Looking diligently lest any man fail of the grace of God ; lest any root of bitterness springing up trouble you, and thereby many be defiled ', the sense of which, and even more that of Deut. xxix. 18, from which it is taken, is not unlike that of our present passage. Others take the reference to be to S. Paul's metaphor of the wild olive, the heathen, grafted into the sweet olive, the redeemed. Others again take the word in a passive sense, ' becoming sweet ' towards them, ' bestowing His sweetness ' on them, but this appears to me difficult to reconcile with the form of a verb in -αινω.

l. 22. *beheaded.* The meaning of this word is much disputed. The subst. τύμπανον means ' a drum ', and is also used, from their resemblance to a drum, for a piece of wood to which those about to be beaten were fastened, for the horse (*equuleus*) on which prisoners were stretched as a torture, and for a stick or cudgel, because the sufferer was beaten like a drum. The verb, simple or compounded with ἀπό, similarly denotes—(1) *to hang up* a prisoner to be beaten ; (2) *to stretch on the horse* ; (3) *to beat to death* ; and (4) *to behead*, perhaps from the resemblance of the block to a drum. It is also alleged that it can be used (5) in a general sense, *to put to death*. The choice here lies, I think, between (3), which is the meaning usually given to it in Heb. xi. 35 (R.V. marg.), and (4). Beating to death, *fustuarium*, was a Roman punishment applied to deserters, and to the martyr S. Valerian, husband of S. Cecilia, and Canon Mason so translates ἀποτυμπανίζω here, but it seems unlikely that the governor would have deliberately set aside the Emperor's instructions (but v. Int. p. 55). '*Beheaded*' falls in with the actual fate of all the Roman citizens (except Attalus) recorded in the next sentence, and is supported by Rufinus, the old Latin translator of Eusebius (*c.* A.D. 400) and by Chrysostom (*in Heb. hom.* 27. 2). (For a full discussion v. Suicer, *Thesaurus*, τυμπανίζω).

l. 24. *festival.* This festival took place on Aug. 1st, the day on which an altar had been dedicated to the Emperor Augustus at Lyons ; v. Suetonius, *Claud.* ii. 1. This, therefore, was the day of martyrdom of SS. Blandina and her companions. They are commemorated however on Jan. 2nd, possibly the day on which the Bishop Pothinus, or some of those who died earlier, suffered.

l. 26. *gazing-stock :* θεατρίζων the verb used in Heb. x. 33, 'whilst ye were made a gazing-stock both by reproaches and afflictions'.

l. 28. *beheaded.* This was the legal punishment for Roman citizens.

PAGE 66, l. 1. *wedding garment :* Matt. xxii. 11–13 ; cf. § 55. There is no doubt an allusion to the white garment (chrisom) worn at baptism.

l. 3. *conversation :* ἀναστροφή, 'conversation', 'manner of life', a common word in the New Testament ; e. g. James iii. 13.

blasphemed the Way : from 2 Peter ii. 2, 'Many shall follow their pernicious ways ; by reason of whom the way of truth shall be evil spoken of', where the Greek word for 'evil spoken of' is the same as that used here, βλασφημέω. For the special interest in quotations from the second Epistle of S. Peter see note on p. 65, l. 7. 'The Way' is the earliest name for the Christian religion ; see Acts ix. 2, 'If he (Saul) found any that were of the Way (R.V.)', so xix. 9, xxii. 4 ; xxiv. 14, 'After the Way which they call a sect' (R.V.), *id.* 22. It is *the* Way to salvation through Jesus Christ, who is 'the Way and the Truth and the Life' (John xiv. 6).

sons of perdition : 2 Thess. ii. 3, 'Except . . . that man of sin be revealed, the son of perdition' ; John xvii. 12 'None of them is lost but the son of perdition.'

l. 6. *Alexander, Phrygian by birth :* cf. note on p. 59, l. 16.

l. 9. *boldness :* the same word which is found in Philemon 8, 'Though I might be much bold (lit. " have much boldness ") in Christ to enjoin thee that which is convenient', cf. 1 John ii. 28 ; iii. 21 (where it is translated ' confidence ') &c. Cf. note on p. 51. 29.

l. 10. *Apostolic gift :* χάρισμα, a gift or grace from God ; e. g. Rom. xii. 6, 'Having then gifts differing according to the grace that is given to us' ; *id.* vi. 23, 'The gift of God is eternal life through Jesus Christ our Lord'. It is particularly used of the special Charismata found in the Corinthian Church (1 Cor. xii. 4), such as the gift of tongues.   The Apostleship heads the list of *Charismata* in 1 Cor. xii. 28.   The Apostolic gift of which the writer is thinking here seems to be that of delivering the Message, the Good News.   Cf. p. 51, l. 15.

l. 13. *as one in travail:* he was bringing forth new children, new disciples for Christ ; cf. Gal. iv. 19, ' My little children, of whom I travail in birth again until Christ be formed in you.'

l. 16. *ordered him to be set before him :* the Greek may mean equally well ' turned his attention to him ' (cf. Arist. *Hist. An.* 1. 1. 12 and other passages quoted in L. & S.) ;

l. 21. *for the second time.*   This was absolutely illegal in the case of a Roman, and contrary to the Emperor's command ; v. p. 65, l. 22.

l. 24. *offered up :* no doubt their throats were cut ; v. *Mart. Perp.* xxi, p. 91.   Some would translate here and in § 40, ' were put to death by the sword ', but the notion of sacrifice is present ; v. next note.

l. 28. *rising upward :* as an offering of his martyrdom to God. Some have remarked as strange the silence about any demand for sacrifice to Caesar in these Acta, but the insistence on the sacrifice they were making to God implies a contrast to the sacrifice they were asked to make to men.

PAGE **67**, l. 10. *sister :* sister in the faith probably, though some think in blood.

l. 13. *like a noble mother :* Knopf gives a reference to the mother and her seven sons who were put to death with tortures by King Antiochus for refusing to eat swine's flesh, 2 Macc. vii. esp. vv. 5, 21–3, 27–9, 41.   The word τήγανον, ' frying pan ', in § 56 is found also in vii. 5 of 2 Macc. . . . It is another name for the red hot chair of § 38, in which the verb translated ' roasted ' (τηγανιζόμενα) is formed from the same word τήγανον.

l. 20. *net.*   The word γυργαθός is used in Aristotle, *H.A.* v. 27. 4, of a spider's web, hence it is used here for ' net ' (Ruf. ' reticulo inclusa '). So SS. Perpetua and Felicitas are enclosed in nets (*Mart. Perp. et Fel.*, xx) before being thrown to the mad heifer.

l. 22. *no further sense :* cf. *Mart. Perp. et Fel.* xx, where S. Perpetua, after being tossed by the heifer, says : ' when we are to be thrown to that heifer I cannot tell '.

l. 30. *wild Beast :* the Devil (cf. ch. ii, § 6) whether imagined as a lion, v. ch., i, § 25 ; ii, § 6), or as a serpent, ' antiquus serpens ' (Rufinus, *c.* A. D. 400).

PAGE **68**, l. 1. ' *He that is wicked* ', &c.: Rev. xxii. 11 ; cf. Dan. xii. 10.

l. 9. *gnashed their teeth :* cf. Acts vii. 54, ' They gnashed on him (Stephen) with their teeth ' ; cf. this Epistle, i. 15.

l. 22. *the martyrs' loss of burial :* S. Augustine refers to this passage (vol. vi, Ben. Ed.) *de cura pro mortuis agenda*, ch. vi, § 8 ;

ch. viii, § 10. This cruelty, he says, was permitted by God 'that Christians might learn in confessing Christ, while they despise this life, to despise still more burial'.

PAGE 69, l. 9. *being in the form of God, &c.*: Phil. ii. 6.

l. 16. *called them martyrs.* The title 'martyrs' was sometimes, but wrongly, given to those who had suffered torture for Christ and had survived : an instance is found in Eusebius, *Hist. Eccl.*, v. 19, where Aurelius, a confessor, speaks of himself as 'Martyr'.

l. 18. *faithful and true witness :* Rev. iii. 14, 'These things saith the Amen, the faithful and true witness' ; Rev. i. 5, 'Jesus Christ, who is the faithful Witness, and the first-begotten of the dead, and the Prince of the kings of the earth' ; Acts iii. 15, 'And (ye) killed the Prince of life'.

l. 26. *made perfect :* cf. Luke xiii. 32, 'The third day I shall be perfected'. The word is often used of the death of martyrs ; cf. Eusebius, *Hist. Eccl.* iii. 35, 'Symeon having been perfected in the manner already described' ; *id.* vii. 15, and *Acts of SS. Carpus, Papylus, and Agathonica,* § 47.

l. 33. *humbled themselves :* 1 Pet. v. 6, 'Humble yourselves therefore under the mighty hand of God, that He may exalt you in due time.'

l. 35. *a reason for their faith to all :* Valesius (a famous editor of Eusebius) has 'omnium defensionem suscipiebant', '*They undertook the defence of all*' ; this makes a better antithesis, but it is very doubtful whether the Greek can bear this interpretation.

PAGE 70, l. 1. *loosed, &c.* These are technical terms of the Sacrament of Penance (cf. Matt. xvi. 19 and xviii. 18, 'whatsoever ye shall bind on earth shall be bound in heaven : and whatsoever ye shall loose on earth shall be loosed in heaven'). The good offices of the martyrs, here shown in persuading the lapsed to a change of mind and promising them forgiveness if they confessed their faith, were in S. Cyprian's time (*c.* A. D. 250) solicited, by those who had lapsed, and only repented after the danger was past (v. S. Cyprian, *Epist.*, x. and xx), to procure their reconciliation with the Church. Sometimes as these letters show, martyrs and confessors claimed of themselves to reconcile the lapsed.

l. 3. *Lord, lay not this sin, &c :* Acts vii. 60 : (for their prayer cf. Eus. *Mart. Pal.* viii. 9–12) : S. Stephen's words are applied to their lapsed brethren as well as to their persecutors.

l. 6. *This :* i.e. the struggle to bring the lapsed to repentance.

l. 8. *the Devil :* cf. 1 Pet. v. 8, 'your adversary the devil, as a roaring lion, walketh about, seeking whom he may devour', and this Epistle, i. 25, 57.

l. 9. *For they did not boast, &c.* There is no suggestion here, as the whole context shows, of a ' Treasury of Merits ', i.e. that the merit of the martyrs was so great, that part could be applied to satisfaction for the sins of others ; v. Routh's note here.

l. 12. *tender mercy* : lit. ' bowels ' ; cf. 1 John iii. 17, ' Bowels of compassion,' &c.

l. 14. *They asked for life, &c. :* cf. Ps. xxi. 4, ' He asked life of Thee, and Thou gavest him a long life : even for ever and ever.'

l. 18. *their Mother :* i. e. the Church.

l. 24. *members of Christ :* cf. 1 Cor. xii. 27, ' Now ye are the body of Christ, and members in particular.' In this sentence Eusebius is referring to harsh treatment by other Christians towards the lapsed in later times, e. g. by the Novatianists, the Puritans of the middle of the third century, who refused all pardon, even on their deathbeds, to the lapsed. They were still to be found in Eusebius's time (beginning of the fourth century).

V. THE ACTS OF THE SCILLITAN SAINTS

PAGE **71**. l. 5. *Saturninus.* Tertullian tells us (*ad. Scap.* 3) that Saturninus was the ' first to draw the sword ' on the Christians in Africa, and that he was punished by the loss of his eyesight.

l. 14. *genius.* The ' genius ' of a man was a kind of guardian spirit which came into being with him, and was the soul, or divine part of him, which lasted after death. Each place too had its ' genius ' (' genius loci ') and the ' genius Romae ' was honoured as early as 218 B.C. The ' genius ' of the Emperor was associated with the worship of the Household Gods of each family after the battle of Actium (31 B.C.). The worship of the Emperor's ' genius ' in life, as embodying that of the Roman people, served as an introduction to his deification after death.

l. 17. *the mystery of simplicity.* The word μυστήριον (' mysterium ') was used by the Greeks of secret beliefs and rites, in which only ' the initiated ' took part, the Mysteries of Eleusis being the most famous. So the Christians used it of supernatural doctrines, hidden from the world and revealed to Christian believers, v. Matt. xiii. 11. ' It is given unto you to know the mysteries of the kingdom of heaven, but to them it is not given,' ' The revelation of the mystery which was kept secret since the world began ' (Rom. xvi. 25), ' The mystery of the gospel ' (Eph. vi. 19), ' The mystery of the faith ' (1 Tim. iii. 9), and many other places in the New Testament. The passage which comes nearest to that of the text is 1 Tim. iii. 16, ' The mystery of godliness,' i.e. of a Christian life. The word is also used in

Christian literature of the Sacraments, and in particular of the Sacrament of the Altar (cf. 'Those holy mysteries' in 3rd Exhortation Communion Service B.C.P.). In the word 'simplicity' Speratus is of course referring to the words of Saturninus immediately preceding, but he is also no doubt thinking of its Christian meaning; v. esp. 2 Cor. xi. 3, 'I fear lest ... your mind should be corrupted from the simplicity (singleness of aim) that is in Christ' (cf. 2 Cor. i. 12, Eph. vi. 5, where the Vulgate has 'in simplicitate'). Speratus has chosen two words, both of which are applicable to the pagan religion, but in an infinitely deeper and truer sense to the Christian.

PAGE 72, l. 5. *whom no man, &c.:* 1 Tim. vi. 16.

l. 7. *the tax:* i. e. the 'portorium', the tax paid on goods imported into a country. Smuggling was as common then as now.

l. 10. *this persuasion:* cf. Gal. v. 8, 'This persuasion cometh not of him that calleth you' (where the Vulgate has the same word 'persuasio' as we have here), both the Latin and the English word being used in the sense of 'opinion', 'belief'.

l. 31. *case:* probably a box for holding books which had been confiscated at the time of their arrest, and was then in court, Mason translates 'bookshelves', but this seems less likely. The question is addressed to them all.

l. 32. *The Books:* probably the Gospels. According to the text of Baronius, the proconsul asks them what are the books they worship, and Speratus answers: 'The four Gospels of our Lord Jesus Christ, and the Epistles of the Apostle S. Paul, and all Scripture inspired by God.' This is the earliest mention of a Latin version of the Bible.

PAGE 73, l. 17. *Laetantius:* the Greek text has 'Celestinus'.

VI. PASSION OF SS. PERPETUA AND FELICITAS

PAGE 78, l. 1. *testified to the grace of God:* Acts xx. 24, 'That I might finish my course with joy ... to testify the gospel of the grace of God.'

l. 12. *later than the last:* lit. 'more last', a combination of comparative and superlative. Tertullian, the probable author (v. Introd.) of the beginning and conclusion of these Acts, is fond of such forms, e.g. 'extremior' 'extremissimus'; a well-known example of the same combination in Greek occurs in Eph. iii. 8, $\dot{\epsilon}\lambda\alpha\chi\iota\sigma\tau\sigma\tau\acute{\epsilon}\rho\omega$. 'Less than the least of all saints' (lit. 'more least').

l. 14. *In the last days, &c.:* Acts ii. 17–18 (Joel ii. 28 foll.).

l. 24. *as the Lord dealt:* cf. 1 Cor. xii. 6 (which is evidently in the writer's mind); also Rom. xii. 3, 1 Cor. vii. 17.

l. 25. *to the glory of God.* The great end of persecution is said by Tertullian to be ‘the glory of God’ ; v. *de Fuga* 1, ‘In persecutions the whole issue is the Glory of God, who approves or rejects, setteth up and setteth down,’ and elsewhere in the same book.

l. 30. *what we have . . . handled :* 1 John i. 1 and 3, ‘What we have heard, what . . . *our hands have handled.* . . declare we unto you, that ye also may have fellowship with us : and truly our fellowship is with the Father, and with His Son Jesus Christ.’ The author (probably Tertullian, v. Introd.) has not only given a new application to the passage, but has written ‘we have handled’ instead of ‘our hands have handled’ : curiously the same misquotation occurs in Tert. *adv. Prax.* 15. The author is appealing to his own generation, whom he calls ‘brothers’, who were in some cases eyewitnesses of the martyrdom, and a younger generation now growing up, whom he calls ‘little children’, ‘filioli’, in allusion to 1 John ii. 1. The language used shows that the writer was a contemporary and that the Acts were compiled within a few years after the Martyrdom (Rob.).

PAGE **79,** l. 4. *Revocatus, &c.* All the names given in these Acts can be parallelled from African inscriptions (Harris’s note).

l. 13. *When I was still, &c.* The Greek version, ἡμῶν παρατηρουμένων, would suggest the meaning ‘while we were still under observation (but not arrested) ’.

l. 23. *pluck out my eyes :* a proverbial expression : cf. Gal. iv. 15, ‘Ye would have plucked out your own eyes.’

l. 24. *annoying me.* The Lat. is ‘vexavit’, which might mean ‘striking me’ (Holsten) or ‘shaking me’ (Bindley), but the word ‘tantum’ ‘only’ suggests, I think, something milder. The Greek version has κράξας, the Shorter Latin ‘exclamans’ i.e. ‘uttered an exclamation’.

l. 29. *after the holy water.* For the first prayer after Baptism cf. Tert. *de Bapt.* 20, ‘When you go up from the most holy bath of your new birthday, and spread forth your hands in prayer in church for the first time with your brethren, ask of the Father, ask of the Lord.’

l. 33. *Rough handling.* The technical sense of *concussura* is unjust accusation for the sake of extortion, and so the Greek takes it here. But the sense here seems to be ‘rough treatment’ with a view to extortion ; and payment was actually made, *inf.* ‘paid for us to be removed ’. Such payments were common : cf. *Constitutions of the Apostles,* v. 1. ‘Of your sweat and labour send to him (the imprisoned Christian) the means whereby he may be fed and pay the soldiers, that his troubles may be lightened, and he may receive proper care.’ (Rob. and H.).

l. 35. Benedictus, *blessed*, is frequently used of martyrs, bishops, and even of Christian women (Tert. *de cultu fem.* ii. 9).

PAGE 80, l. 4. *My baby, &c.* This comes in the Greek text and appears to be necessary to the sense. S. Perpetua is clearly at first separated from her child, she is 'tortured by anxiety' for him (see above), and finds him 'already faint for want of food'.

l. 12. *my prison.* The sentence gains a new point, as Robinson notices, if we remember that the prison was part of the palace of the proconsul on the Byrsa, or citadel of Carthage.

l. 22. *brazen :* according to another manuscript 'golden'.

ladder : an allusion no doubt to Jacob's ladder, Gen. xxviii. 12. In the Acts of Montanus and Lucius (ch. vii) which are 'a base imitation' of this Martyrdom, the Lord says : 'Give them the sign of Jacob' (Rob.)

l. 29. *dragon :* Satan : cf. Rev. xii. 9, &c.

l. 33. *of his own building :* lit. 'he had himself edified us', *aedificaverat*) ; cf. 1 Cor. xiv. 4, 1 Thess. v. 11.

PAGE 81, l. 5. *trod on his head.* Victor Vitensis A. D. 450–500 (*de persec. Vandal.* i. 3.) mentions that the Vandals spared the Basilica where the bodies of SS. Perpetua and Felicitas and the Scillitan martyrs (v. p. 71) were buried. The frontispiece shows the inscription recently discovered in Carthage on the site of the Passion of S. Perpetua and her fellow martyrs. There is no doubt an allusion to the promise in Gen. iii. 15, 'And I will put enmity between thee and the woman, and between thy seed and her seed ; it shall bruise thy head, and thou shalt bruise his heel,' cf. ch. x. *inf.*

l. 7. *with white hair :* an allusion to Rev. i. 13–14, 'one like unto the Son of man ... His head and His hairs were white like wool, as white as snow.'

a shepherd : our Lord ; cf. John x. 11, 14, 16.

l. 8. *clad in white :* other martyrs ; cf. Rev. vii. 13, 14.

l. 11. *milk :* lit. 'cheese'.

l. 12. *joined hands :* 'The natural action to catch the dripping morsel' (Rob.) in the 'joined' or 'crossed hands', but there is no doubt also an allusion to the reception of the Eucharist.

l. 13. *Amen.* 'Amen' was and is said *by the recipient* at the Eucharist, but no instance is known of its being said by others. Harris believes (as had already occurred to me before I read his note) that the allusion is to the 'Amen' to the Prayer of Consecration, of which S. Paul speaks, 1 Cor. xiv. 16, 'Else how could the unlearned say the Amen at thy Thanksgiving.' He adds that the Fathers commonly spoke of the Amen as a shout, so that we need not be surprised that at this point S. Perpetua awoke. In the *Teaching of the Apostles* (x. 6) the Amen follows, instead of preceding, the Reception, but, apart from this, it must be remembered that S. Perpetua is narrating a vision, which, though it recalls the Eucharist in some particulars, does not represent it exactly, nor follow its order. So the Vision of ch. viii, if it refers to Baptism, which is disputed, is no exact picture of the Baptismal Rite. For it is of the nature of a vision to convey a truth through a Divine message, not literally but in a figure. The facts of real life may colour, but do not bind or limit its meaning. Here the picture of the Good Shepherd is the directing thought, the thought of the Eucharist is secondary. The milk given her is from Him, as are the bread and wine of the Eucharist. There may be also a reminiscence of Baptism, which she had just received (ch. iii). That milk was given after Baptism (Tert. *de Cor.* 3 and *adv. Marc.* i. 14), and sometimes with the first communion (v. Canon 24 of the 3rd council of Carthage A.D. 397), may have influenced the form of the vision. Another thought is the witness of the Faithful, represented by the familiar Amen of the Consecration Prayer.

l. 19. *the hill :* cf. ch. iii and note. The prison was part of the Praetorium, or proconsular palace on the Byrsa, or Acropolis, the city being on the plain below ; the remains of the palace can still be traced.

l. 32. *lady :* cf. ch. iv, beg. An equivalent title of respect is given to brothers and sons in epitaphs, e. g. 'Filio et domino meo' (Rob.).

PAGE **82,** l. 10. *the step :* i. e. which led from the floor of the court to the tribunal on which the judge and prisoners were.

l. 11. The procurator had charge of the imperial revenues in Africa, which was a Senatorial province.

l. 19. *the judge :* or possibly, as the Greek version says, one of the guard.

l. 24. *in great joy.* This joy in martyrdom was quite unfeigned. Marcus Aurelius, *Meditations,* xi. 3, alludes to it, attributing it to 'perversity'. Mensurius, Bishop of Carthage, had to forbid his flock from rushing on martyrdom.

PAGE **83,** l. 1. *was entitled :* as one destined to martyrdom.

l. 12. *a great gulf.* There is no doubt an allusion to Luke xvi. 26, the parable of Dives and Lazarus, though the word is not the same.

l. 18. *he could not drink.* 'The boy no doubt had died unbaptized, and this was the cause of his appearing to be in a place of torment' (Rob.'s note). He adds that S. Augustine (*de an. ad Renatum,* i. 10) challenges this view and holds that his appearance in a place of punishment (i. e. Purgatory) was due to sin committed after baptism. 'For boys of that age can already lie and speak truth, confess or deny (i. e. offer to idols).'

l. 23. *Geta.* The name of Geta is found in only one manuscript. Caracalla put to death any one who wrote, or even uttered the name of Geta, whom he murdered A.D. 212, hence probably its erasion in other manuscripts.

l. 26. *the stocks.* This was an unusual severity (Rob. note), v. note on p. 84, l. 3 and *Letter of Churches of Vienne and Lyons*, i. 27 and note.

l. 31. *poured water :* translating the Greek ἔρρεεν ὕδωρ ; the Lat. here is corrupt.

l. 33. *began to drink from it, &c.* This imagery suggests, if Rob.'s view be taken (v. *sup.*), his need of baptism, cf. the similarly symbolic treatment of the Eucharist in ch. iv ; if S. Augustine's, his cleansing from sins committed on earth, and remission of further punishment in answer to his sister's prayer. There is a difficulty about either view— that he should have been baptized in a heathen household is improbable, on the other hand it is contrary to the traditional Catholic belief that his condition, if he were unbaptized, could be changed. He would be happy, but in the limbo of infants.

PAGE 84, l. 3. *adjutant :* Lat. *optio,* a very common word in the African inscriptions, used for any lieutenant of a higher officer : they had been transferred (v. ch. vii) to the military prison. S. Ambrose, *in Ep. ad Eph.* iv. 11–12 has *optio carceris.* The codex Bezae has *optio* for the jailor in Acts xvi. 23, 27, 36. Pudens at first treats them badly. He keeps them in the stocks in the daytime, an act of unusual severity (ch. viii.) Here he shows signs of softening. Afterwards he believes (ch. xvi), and in ch. xxii Saturus encourages him to make his faith perfect (v. Rob. note).

l. 17. *white robe ... curiously wrought : multiplices,* lit. ' manifold ', Gr. ποικίλα, which suggests my rendering : cf. p. 85, l. 2. The epitaph of Abercius (*c.* A.D. 200) describes the Church of Rome as wearing golden slippers : cf. also Song of Songs vii. 1, and Isa. lii. 7. He wears white as a sign of his approaching martyrdom, cf. *sup.* ch. iv, and Rev. vii. 13–14. Ruinart in his note says that the *discincta* (ungirdled tunic) was a garment open in front, like an academical B.A. or M.A. gown : cf. *inf.,* p. 85, l. 1, and *Passion of SS James and Marian,* ch. vii.

l. 28. *an Egyptian :* the Devil, v. end of this chapter ; so called because of the oppression which the Chosen People suffered in Egypt ; cf. Rev. xi. 8, where Jerusalem, where our Lord and His followers were persecuted, is spoken of as ' the great city, which spiritually is called Sodom and Egypt, where also our Lord was crucified '.

l. 31. *changed into a man :* i. e. that she might take the part of a combatant in the arena.

l. 34. *sand : afa* or *haphe* (Mart. *Epigr.* vii. 67, Sen. *Ep.* 57), Gr.

ἀφή, the technical word for the yellow sand with which wrestlers after being anointed were sprinkled. There is no doubt an allusion (Rob., Introd.) to Gen. iii. 14, 'Dust shalt thou eat all the days of thy life.'

a man : probably Our Lord. Ruinart compares Clement of Alexandria who says (*str.* vii. 3, p. 839) that in the Christian warfare ' the Father is the President, the Son of God the Judge (our Greek version here has the same word, βραβευτής), and the spectators are the Angels ' (cf. Heb. xii. 1.).

PAGE **85,** l. 1. *two stripes :* Senators wore a broad purple stripe (*clavus*), Knights a narrow. This clavus is frequently represented in ancient Christian frescoes and mosaics. Nearly all representations of Apostles, and many of Angels, have it. In a mosaic of S. Agatha Major at Ravenna Our Lord wears a pallium with clavus of gold. The stripes are broader or narrower according to the dignity of the wearer, e. g. Our Lord wears a broader clavus than the Apostles, and priests (probably) than deacons. In nearly all cases the clavi are two in number, running from each shoulder to the lower border of the dress. There are a few examples of a single *clavus* running down the centre of the breast. The stripes are found on other garments besides the tunic, e. g. on the pallium, v. *sup.* (*Dict. of Christ. Antiq.*, Clavus). The readings here vary, and the rendering is very doubtful. Our Lord may be wearing purple as a King, or, as Ruinart suggests, because in the vision he appears as the *gymnasiarchus* or judge of the games, and the *gymnasiarchus* was usually dressed in purple (Luc., *de gymn.* 3).

ll. 10–16. *With my heels . . . trod upon his head :* an allusion to Gen. iii. 15, 'And I will put enmity between thee and the woman, and between thy seed and her seed ; it shall bruise thy head, and thou shalt bruise his heel ' (cf. ch. iv. *sup.*) The Vulgate rendering ' Ipsa conteret,' ' she shall bruise,' adds a further point (Rob.) For a similar reference cf. Epiphanius, *Panarion* 2, 69, 81, 'We trod on the serpent, and we bruised the head of the dragon by the power of God.'

l. 20. *Gate of Life.* This was the name of one of the gates of the amphitheatre, v. *inf.* ch. xx, which led to the forum, to which combatants whom the people spared, especially victorious combatants, retired, in contrast to the ' porta Libitinensis,' or Gate of Death, through which the dead bodies of gladiators were carried on the bier (libitina). To S. Perpetua it has, of course, a special significance.

l. 31. *looking upward :* ' Head downward ' (Rob.).

l. 32. *the world below :* lit. ' the first world '.

PAGE **86,** l. 4. *leaves sang :* adopting an attractive conjecture of Rob., ' canebant ' *sang* for ' cadebant ' *fell* : compare Isa. xliv. 23, ' Sing, O ye heavens ; for the Lord hath done it, shout, ye lower parts of the earth : break forth into singing, ye mountains, O forest, and every tree therein,' also 1 Chron. xvi. 33 ; Isa. xxxv. 1–2, lv. 12, and a passage from the *History of Barlaam and Josaphat*, p. 280 foll., describing Paradise, in which ' the leaves of the trees made a tuneful sound '. This passage in its earlier form may have been known to S. Saturus.

l. 5. *four angels :* perhaps Michael, Gabriel, Raphael, and Uriel, four Archangels.

l. 10. *violets :* adopting another conjecture of Rob., ' violatum ', suggested by the reading of one MS. ' violata ' : the other MSS. have ' via lata,' ' by a wide road.'

l. 20. *Holy, holy, holy :* Isa. vi. 3. The words in the text are Greek ' Agios (ἄγιος), agios, agios ' in place of the usual ' Sanctus, sanctus, sanctus ' of the Latin, ' Holy, holy, holy ' of our Canon of the Mass. The Greek form (along with other Greek words) is still found in the Latin service of Reproaches on Good Friday, *Agios O Theos* (O holy God) : *Agios ischyros* (ἰσχυρός) (O holy strong One) : *Agios athanatos eleison imas* (ἀθάνατος, ἐλέησον ἡμᾶς) (O holy immortal One have mercy upon us). Another Greek form still surviving in Western service books is the familiar *Kyrie eleison* (κύριε ἐλέησον) ' Lord have mercy upon us '.

l. 22. *white as snow :* cf. Rev. i. 14. (Dan. vii. 9), ' His head and His hairs were white like wool, as white as snow.' He adds, I think, ' His feet we saw not,' because the description of Christ's feet in that ch. ' His feet like unto fine brass as if they burned in a furnace ' might be expected to be repeated here. It is possible, however, that S. Saturus is contrasting his vision with that of S. Perpetua in ch. x. where she describes the shoes worn by Our Lord (Harris on ch. x.).

l. 27. *stroked our faces with His hand :* Rob. suggests a reminiscence of Rev. vii. 17, ' God shall wipe away all tears from their eyes ' ; the Latin phrase here is very obscure, ' De manu sua traiecit nobis in faciem.'

l. 28. *the other :* i. e. the larger number behind the silent eight on guard.

l. 29. *Kiss of Peace :* cf. note on ch. xxi.

l. 35. *priest-teacher.* In the early Church the offices of Priest and Preacher were distinguished : in Alexandria at one time priests were forbidden to preach. Cyprian, however, (c. A.D. 250), *Ep.* xxix, speaks of priest-teachers. It was not till the establishment of the parochial system that they were regularly combined.

PAGE 87, l. 3. *left us thus :* i. e. still quarrelling, and outside the gate.

l. 6. *talk Greek.* This suggests that the original version of the Martyrdom was (v. Introd.) in Latin.

l. 13. *like men returning from the circus.* The usual number of

chariots starting for each race was four, and the drivers were divided
into four *factiones*, the Green, the Red, the Blue, and the White.
Heavy bets were laid on this or that 'faction', and the contests
sometimes led to bloody riots. The famous Nika Sedition of the
Blues and Greens in A.D. 532 nearly cost Justinian his crown.

l. 24. *his body . . . made acquaintance with the sword :* his body,
that is to say, was mangled after his death. Cf. *The Martyrs of
Lyons*, i. 62, where their bodies are said to have been 'made a show of
in all kinds of ways'. He may, however, have been beheaded in
prison, and the reference may be to Matt. x. 28 (so Rob.). The Greek
version, which has 'The sword pierced if not through his soul at all
events through his flesh', clearly supposed that there was a reference to
Luke ii. 35, 'Yea, a sword shall pierce through thy own soul also,' but
the connexion is difficult to see.

PAGE 88, l. 6. *one of the warders : cataractariorum. Cataracta* is
properly a *cataract*, e.g. the great Cataract of the Nile, then a *portcullis*.
It is found in the Septuagint and Theodotian's version of Jer. xx. 2,
where Jerome has 'nervum', possibly in the sense of 'prison', from
the barred gates, resembling a portcullis. 'Cataractarii' would then
mean, as here translated, 'warders,' as apparently in the *Acts of SS.
Montanus and Lucius*, ch. xvii (Ruinart, p. 280). 'Cataracta' may,
however, mean 'stocks' in the above passage of Jeremiah (so the A.V.
and R.V.), which were sometimes used for torture (cf. *Letter of the
Churches of Vienne and Lyons*, i. 27), in which case 'cataractarii'
would mean 'keepers of the stocks' or 'torturers' (from Ruinart,
Ducange, and Forcellini).

l. 18. *sacred bequest :* Lat. *fidei commissum*, which implies 'a
sacred trust of moral rather than of legal obligation' (Rob.), dependent
on a request.

l. 23. *carried off from prison by some magic spells.* Is this fear due
to remembrance still surviving of S. Peter's and the Apostles' escapes
from prison (Acts xii. 7, v. 19), and the opening of the doors of S.
Paul's and S. Silas's prison at Philippi (Acts xvi. 26) ?

l. 25. *most noble* (nobilissimus) is a constant epithet for a Caesar,
transferred here to the condemned persons who are to suffer on his
festival, and share in his honour (from Rob.'s note).

l. 32. *governor of the prison :* Pudens ; cf. chaps. ix. and xxi.

l. 34. *the free festivity.* The 'libera cena' mentioned in the text
was a feast given to condemned criminals on the night before they
suffered, sumptuous and held in public. Tertullian, probably the
author of this account of the deaths of the martyrs (v. Introd., p. 75),
refers to it *Apol.* 42, 'I do not dine in public at the Liberalia, as is
the custom of fighters with beasts taking their last dinner.'

PAGE 89, l. 1. *love-feast.* The 'Agape' or 'love-feast' was a corporate meal among the early Christians (Acts ii. 42, 46, xx. 7, 11, 1 Cor. xi. 17–34). In the beginning it concluded with the Eucharist, but by the second century it was already distinct from it, and took place in the evening, while the Eucharist was celebrated at the morning meeting. In our earliest account of the manner in which the Holy Communion was celebrated, in the *Apology* of Justin Martyr (*c.* A.D. 150 cf. p. 47), there is no mention of the Agape. Tertullian (born A.D. 160), *Apol.* ch. 39, speaks of it as a modest meal, to which the poor were invited, preceded and concluded by prayer, and accompanied by the singing of psalms and hymns.

l. 14. *true wife of Christ :* cf. Tert., *ad uxor.* i. 4, 'our sisters . . . prefer to wed with God.'

l. 15. *darling of God :* ' Dei delicata,' a bold expression, ' darling ' or ' favourite ', found in inscriptions, e. g. *C. I. L.* Afr. 2861, ' To darling Julia, the well deserving ' (Rob.).

l. 19. *Second Baptism :* i. e. the baptism of blood in martyrdom. An unchristened person dying as a martyr was ' washed in his own blood ', and thereby secured the grace of baptism : cf. ch. xxi.

l. 21. *priests of Saturn.* From the evidence of the inscriptions it is clear that the worship both of Saturn and of Ceres was extremely popular in Africa. Tertullian, *ad uxor.* i. 6, tells us that women were known to have left their husbands to dedicate themselves to the service of the African Ceres. Lactantius (*div. inst.* 6.20) tells us that ' venationes ', fights with beasts, were dedicated to Saturn. The men would have worn scarlet cloaks, the women a fillet round their heads (Tert., *de test. animae*, 2). It was not uncommon to force a Christian prisoner to represent some heathen character or engage in some idolatrous ceremony. So Clement (*ad Cor.* vi.) speaks of Christian women who were compelled to play the parts of Danaids or Dirce in the arena (Harris *in loc.*).

l. 25. *pledged our lives :* ' animum addiximus,' a metaphor from the oath which gladiators who volunteered for the service took when they sold themselves to their trainer (*lanista*) (Rob.).

l. 30. *treading on the head of the Egyptian :* v. Perpetua's vision, ch. x.

l. 33. *Hilarian :* the procurator ; v. ch. vi.

PAGE 90, l. 2. *beast-fighters.* Beside the criminals, often Christians, who were condemned to fight with wild beasts, there were others, known as ' bestiarii ' or ' venatores ' (the word used here), who fought armed for pay, and were trained in schools. They carried long hunting-whips of cowhide, and that it was not uncommon to force criminals to run the gauntlet before them is clear from two passages in Tertullian (*ad mart.* 5 and *ad nat.* i. 18), where some are said to have run through the lines of whips not as a punishment but for money. Cf. *Letter of the Churches of Vienne and Lyons*, p. 63, l. 34. 'They ran the gauntlet of whips according to the custom of the arena' (Holsten).

l. 5. John xvi. 24, 'Ask, and ye shall receive, that your joy may be full.' Matt. vii. 7 (Luke xi. 9) 'Ask, and it shall be given you; seek, and ye shall find; knock, and it shall be opened unto you,' seems also to have been in the writer's mind; cf. also Matt. xxi. 22.

l. 12. *mauled on the platform.* A picture exists (*Rev. Archéol.*, 1889, vol. xiii. p. 155) of a man bound to a post on a platform, and a lion springing to get at him.

l. 16. *the fighter :* one of the professional fighters with beasts.

bound him to the boar. The prisoner, condemned to fight with beasts, was often bound to the beast to prevent his escaping. Sometimes beasts were thus tethered together, as for instance a bear and a bull (Holsten).

l. 19. *tied up on the bridge.* The Emperor Commodus made bridges in the arena from which he might dispatch the beasts (Holsten).

l. 25. *that he wished . . . beast :* I have adopted Mr. Bindley's translation here.

l. 26. *enclosed in nets :* this was also done in the case of S. Blandina (v. p. 67, l. 20.)

l. 34. *asked for a pin :* reading '⟨acu⟩ requisita,' a conjecture in Knopf, which is confirmed by the Gr. ἐπιζητήσασα βελόνην.

PAGE 91, l. 1. *seem to mourn.* Female mourners at Roman funerals had their heads bare and wore their hair dishevelled.

l. 6. *Gate of Life :* v. note on ch. x.

l. 9. *in the Spirit :* cf. Rev. iv. 2, 'And immediately I was in the spirit' (cf. i. 10 ' I was in the Spirit on the Lord's day.')

l. 11. *When we are to be thrown, &c.* ' Where was she,' says S. Augustine (*Serm.* cclxxx. 4),' when she did not know she was fighting with the fierce heifer, and asked when that should happen which had happened already?' Cf. *Letter of Churches of Vienne and Lyons* i. 56, and *Tert. ad mart.* ii.

l. 16. 1 Cor. xvi. 13, 'Watch ye, stand fast in the faith, quit you like men, be strong.'

l. 17. *Be not offended.* There is clearly an allusion to Matt. xiii. 21, ' when tribulation or persecution ariseth because of the word, by and by he is offended,' where the same word ' Scandalizo ' is used in the Vulgate.

l. 19. *Pudens :* v. note, ch. ix.

l. 26. *Second Baptism :* v. note, ch. xviii.

Bless you, &c. In an inscription given by H. from the mosaic of an ancient bath pavement (*C. I. L.*, v. 4500) there occur three traditional sayings addressed by the bathman to the bather : ' Bene lava,' ' bathe well,' before, ' Salvum lotum ' (the phrase here), ' well bathed,' after the bath, and the third which may mean 'take a towel'.

l. 29. *faith and me :* reading ' fidei et mei ', after the Greek.

l. 31. *ring.* The *optiones* of the legion all wore rings ; the ring of Pudens was no doubt official, which he wore as an ' optio ' (H. ch. ix. note).

l. 35. *place allotted to the throat-cutting.* This place was known as the ' Spoliarium ', where those who were taken wounded from the arena were dispatched. Seneca (*Ep.* 93) asks whether we can imagine any one so greedy of life that he would prefer to have his throat cut in the ' spoliarium ' than to die in the arena.

PAGE 92, l. 6. *Pax :* i. e. the Kiss of Peace ; cf. ch. xii. Rock (*Church of our Fathers*, pt. 2, ch. xii) says : ' The Salisbury rubric was to send just before the Communion the " Pax " all about the church. This was conveyed from one to another by a kiss on the cheek.' The custom lasted in England up to the middle of the 13th century, when for the kiss upon the cheek was substituted the kissing of a ' Pax ' of wood or metal, passed from hand to hand. Tertullian (*de orat.* xviii) says, ' what prayer is perfect without the holy kiss ? . . . what sacrifice (in ref. to the Eucharist) from which we depart without the Kiss of Peace ? ' He calls it the ' seal of prayer,' as the sign of Christian Brotherhood. It was specially associated with the Communion.

l. 10. *awaited Perpetua :* cf. ch. iv.

l. 13. *young untried gladiator.* A young gladiator or fighter with beasts was trained for his trade by cutting the throats of wounded combatants in the ' Spoliarium ', v. note above.

l. 16. *called and chosen :* cf. S. Matt. xxii. 14, ' For many are called, but few are chosen.' Rev. xvii. 14, ' They that are with him are called and chosen and faithful.'

l. 17. *glory of Jesus Christ.* Tertullian, the probable author of the Preface and Epilogue (v. Introd., p. 75), insists in his book *Concerning Flight in Persecution* that the great end of persecution is ' the glory of God ', cf. chap. i. and note, ix, xii, xiv.

VII. ACTS OF S. CYPRIAN

PAGE 95, l. 13. *made heaven, &c. :* Exod. xx. 11 ; Acts iv. 24, xiv. 15.

l. 15. *for all men, &c. :* cf. 1 Tim. ii. 1 foll.

l. 23, *Curubis :* a town on the east coast of Tunis, about 50 miles south-east of Carthage.

l. 30. *Delatores*, informers, were encouraged by Augustus, and still more by Tiberius, till they became a public danger. They were banished by Trajan (A.D. 98–117).

PAGE 96, l. 5. *our discipline forbids* : Christians were forbidden to court persecution : cf. *Mart. S. Polycarp*, iv. and Matt. x. 23, John vii. 1 &c. This sentence is quoted by S. Aug. *c. Gaud*. i. 31. 40.

l. 13. The cemeteries, which the Christians had in very early times acquired for themselves that they might not be buried with the heathen, were often used for worship, and especially for the celebration of the Eucharist at the graves of the martyrs.

l. 16. *ordered . . . to be banished.* S. Augustine, *Serm*. 309, repeats this and many other statements from these Acta. This and the four following *Sermons* were delivered ' on the birthday of Cyprian the Martyr '.

l. 25. *divine command* : a quotation from the official records : it would not offend a Christian, remembering 1 Pet. ii 13–14, ' Submit yourselves to every ordinance of man for the Lord's sake : whether it be to the king, as supreme ; or unto governors.'

l. 27. *as had been shown him* : v. Introd. to these Acts, p. 93, for the vision to which this refers.

l. 30. *equerry* : ' strator,' properly a groom who ' sternit ', *saddles*, the horse and helps his master to mount, but generally used of an official, who had as little connexion with his original duties as our ' equerry '. That it was an honourable office is shown by the use of it alone as a title of honour. He was frequently a ' decurio ', or commander of a division of cavalry. He often had charge of prisoners, as appears from a law of Constantine quoted in the Oxford edition of Cyprian. Cf. *marshal*, which originally meant a ' farrier '.

PAGE 97, l. 3. *under guard* : ' ductus,' technically used of a person led to prison.

l. 7. *temple of Public Welfare* : ' Salutaria ', the temple of Salus, the goddess who presided over the welfare of Rome.

l. 19. *Sauciolum* : an obscure word. It was apparently used of the chamber in which prisoners were put to death (v. note in Oxford ed. of Cyprian). There are various readings, Sauciolo, Secutiolo, Saloutio.

l. 24. *Pope* : Lat. papa, meaning *father* from Gk. πάπας. Originally used of all bishops, it became restricted to the Bishop of Rome in the West and of Alexandria, Antioch, Jerusalem, and Constantinople in the East ; it was further restricted to the Bishop of Rome alone by the 9th century, perhaps earlier. In the East it is applied regularly to priests. Cf. p. 87, l. 4, where ' father ' is in the Latin ' papa '.

PAGE 98, ll. 2–13. *You have long lived . . . your blood* : Pontius, one of S. Cyprian's deacons, who wrote his life, regards all these words of the proconsul as prophetic (see Life, ch. xvii) ; 'standard-bearer,' who taught men to bear Christ's sign ; 'enemy of the Gods,' who gave their idols to destruction ; 'an example,' for he was the first of many witnesses ; 'discipline,' not Roman, but Christian, vindicated and established in the blood of the martyrs.

l. 8. *Caesar.* The reigning Emperor, or Emperors, bore the title of Augustus ; the title Caesar was often bestowed on the heir to the throne, or on others associated, but in an inferior position, with the Emperor.

l. 21. *mantle :* 'lacerna byrro,' (or 'birro '). The 'byrrus' was a woollen cloak used for bad weather, 'lacerna' being a general name for such a garment. It was often costly, and seems to have been specially worn by bishops. S. Augustine, *Serm.* 356, says, 'Don't offer me a costly byrrus ; it may suit a bishop, but not a poor man, a poor man's son, like Augustine ' : cf. Palladius, *Hist. Laus.*, ch. lxiii.

l. 23. The dalmatic was a long-sleeved, usually white, tunic with a longitudinal stripe (' clavus ') running downward from either side of the neck. It was in S. Cyprian's time part of the dress of a Roman layman, of a stately and luxurious character, worn by persons in high position. About fifty years later it became the peculiar dress of the deacon.

l. 25. *executioner.* 'Spiculatores ' (' speculatores ') under the Empire formed a special corps and served as a bodyguard to the Emperor. They sometimes acted as executioners ; cf. Mark vi. 27, ' Immediately the king sent an executioner (marg. ' one of his guard ') and commanded his head to be brought.'

l. 28. *golden pieces :* 'aureos.' The 'aureus ' was equal to 25 denarii, 100 sesterces, value roughly £1. So S. Maximilian (*Acta Maximiliani*, ch. iii) instructs his father to give his new uniform to the executioner.

were strewn before him : to be preserved as relics. I have taken the translation from Mason.

l. 32. The subdiaconate is the lowest of the major orders in the Western Church. There are recorded to have been among the Roman clergy just before Cyprian's death 46 priests, seven deacons, and seven subdeacons, and this is the first mention of subdeacons. Cyprian speaks of them in his letters.

PAGE 99, l. 2. *torches :* 'scolacibus,' torches made of rope.

l. 4. Procurator was the general name for the civil servants of the Emperor, from the highest to the lowest.

VIII. ACTS OF SS. FRUCTUOSUS AND HIS DEACONS

PAGE 100, l. 5. *orderlies :* 'beneficiarii,' so called because they owed their position to the favour of the 'tribunus' ('colonel') of the regiment. They were exempt from menial duties, and were attendants on magistrates, acting as court messengers, ushers, policemen.

l. 7. *sound of their feet :* 'pedibulum,' which some interpret of the lictor's rod (so called, they think, from *pedum,* a shepherd's crook).

l. 9. *slippers :* 'soleis,' a kind of sandal, consisting of a sole fastened on by a strap across the instep, worn in the house only.

PAGE 101, l. 12. *made heaven, &c.:* Exod. xx. 11 ; Acts iv. 24, xiv. 15.

l. 27. *Do you worship, &c.:* taking the reading in S. Augustine, *Serm.* 273. 3, 'Numquid et tu Fructuosum colis ?'

l. 28. *I do not worship.* S. Augustine says (*ib.* 5), 'The names of the Martyrs are recited at Christ's altar, but they are not worshipped as Christ ;' cf. id. *c. Faust.* xx. 21 (a very interesting passage).

l. 34. *You were :* 'fuisti,' a regular Latin expression for death ; cf. Cicero's saying after the death of Catiline and his fellow conspirators—Vixerunt, 'They have lived.' It was misread 'fustibus', whence one version states that they were beaten with sticks.

PAGE 102, l. 10. *drugged wine :* Gams (*die Kirchengeschichte von Spanien* i. 267) rejects this translation of 'conditi permixti' ; he regards it as a drink to strengthen, not benumb, and translates 'spiced wine' (cf. Matt. xxvii. 34).

l. 13. *fast :* 'stationem,' a fast, the same as 'jejunium (l. 11)', with this difference that 'statio' is properly used of regular fasts such as Advent and Lent, hence the name because they took place 'statis diebus' (but S. Ambrose says they are called 'stationes' because they are *encampments* which protect us from the attack of the Devil). Wednesday and Friday were *stations,* on these days the fast lasted only till the ninth hour (3 p.m.). These days were sacred because the betrayal was planned on Wednesday and the crucifixion accomplished on Friday.

l. 16. *for them that love Him :* 1 Cor. ii. 9.

l. 19. *Reader :* 'Lector,' the second of the four minor orders, who in the first centuries read all the lessons in the Liturgy, including the Epistle and Gospel ; v. *Martyrdom of S. Procopius,* i.

l. 20. *loose his shoes :* cf. *Mart. Polyc.* xiii. 2.

l. 28. *I must have in mind, &c.* Alexander Lesley, *Praef. Miss. Mixt.* 210 (Migne, *Patrol. Lat.* lxxxv.), considers (and Gams, *Kirch. von Span.* i. 275, agrees) that these words of S. Fructuosus refer to a prayer in the Mozarabic Missal (pp. 3 and 224) at the beginning of Low Mass : ' In our prayers let us have in mind the Holy Catholic Church : that the Lord of His grace may think fit to increase her in faith, hope, and charity.' If so, this passage is of great interest as a proof of the antiquity of this Rite. S. Augustine, *Serm.* 273. 2, says finely in reference to these words : ' If you wish that I should pray for you, do not leave her for whom I pray.' (Cf. *Mart. Polyc.* v).

l. 31. *gate :* so Gams ; Ruinart has ' foro ', open space.

PAGE **103**, l. 5. *when he had comforted the brethren.* Some manu-scripts add that one of the brethren, Martialis, urged him to make a farewell speech.

l. 10. *the Divine Trinity was visible.* Nothing more apparently is meant than that both the *Three* Children (Dan. iii. 19–25) and these *three* martyrs symbolized the Holy Trinity, which was present in the Three Persons to aid on both occasions. So Prudentius, *Peristeph.*, *hymn.* vi. 4–6, says of these three martyrs, ' The Almighty Trinity crowns the Spanish citadel with three martyrs.'

l. 13. *the midst of the fire :* Dan. iii. 25. ' Lo, I see four men loose, walking in the midst of the fire, and they have no hurt ; and the form of the fourth is like the Son of God,' where ' Son of God ' is variously interpreted of the Second Person of the Trinity, or of an Angel.

l. 15. *Divine prayer.* What is meant by ' orationis divinae ' ? Gams translates it ' Command ' (*Gebotes*), but can ' oratio ' mean command ? It seems to me that the reference is either to the prayer of our Lord upon the Cross, ' Father, forgive them, for they know not what they do,' which would fit in with the end of the sentence, or to the Lord's Prayer, but for this the ordinary equivalent is, of course, *oratio Dominica.*

l. 17. *a symbol of the Lord's victory.* They extend their arms on either side of the stake to which they were fastened, recalling our Lord on the Cross. Prudentius, *Peristeph.*, *hymn.* vi. 106, ' Punishment dared not bind their hands, that are to be raised in the form of a cross to the Father.'

l. 24. *according to the flesh :* cf. *Letter of the Churches of Vienne and Lyons,* i. 18 and note.

PAGE **104**, ll. 14–19. The passage in brackets is clearly a later addition, as Gams notes (*Kirch. von Span.* i. 269). It is absurd that Aemilian who was unworthy to see the vision of Babylas and Mygdonius should now have a vision of his own ; and it is quite alien to the spirit of these Acta that the martyred Fructuosus should ' chide and mock ' him. This conclusion is rendered almost certain by the fact that Prudentius, who gives the whole substance of the

Acta in his Sixth Hymn, omits this, ending with the burial of the Martyrs' relics.

l. 22. *crown that fadeth not away :* 1 Pet. v. 4.

l. 23. *trod under foot,* &c. : cf. *Mart. Perp. et Felic.,* iv.

IX. PASSION OF SS. JAMES AND MARIAN

PAGE **107,** l. 5. *the common bond of the Gospel :* 'sacramenti,' the equivalent of the Greek μυστήριον, *mystery.* Hence it was used not only for what we call 'sacraments', but also for revealed truths about Divine things, and Christian writers spoke of the 'Sacramentum' of the Trinity or of the Incarnation. So the Creed is 'Sacramentum religionis'. Here 'The Gospel' seems the nearest equivalent, comparing Rom. xvi. 25, 'According to my Gospel, and the preaching of Jesus Christ, according to the revelation of the mystery' (where the Old Latin version has 'sacramenti'), and 1 Cor. ii. 7 'we speak the wisdom of God in a mystery' (where S. Hilary reads 'in sacramento.')

l. 23. *welcome duties.* The writer probably refers to his own confession, ch. iv, and his support of the martyrs during their imprisonment and sufferings.

l. 26. *Cirta :* the chief city in Numidia, and a Roman colony with the surname *Julia.* It was restored by Constantine and called Constantina, the name it still bears (Constantine.)

l. 29. *this present world :* 'saeculi,' the present evil world : it is used in this sense in the Vulgate, e. g. James iv. 4, 'Whosoever . . . will be a friend of the world is the enemy of God.'

PAGE **108,** l. 14. *Secundinus :* perhaps the bishop who is one of those who subscribed to the Synodical Letter written to the Church of Rome on the question of the lapsed (Cyprian, *Ep.* lvii (liv.)).

l. 18. *from punishment to punishment.* They had been banished from their sees, and were probably among the nine Numidian bishops condemned to the mines at Sigus near Cirta.

l. 22. Cf. 1 Cor. xv. 55, 'O death, where is thy sting ?'

l. 35. *charity . . . love.* 'Caritas' is the theological virtue of *charity* (1 Cor. xiii), 'that habit or power which disposes us to love God above all creatures for Himself, and to love ourselves and our neighbours for the sake of God' (*Cath. Enc.,* art. 'Charity ').

'dilectio,' is a general term for *love,* common in the Vulgate, e. g. John xiii. 35, 'By this shalt all men know that ye are my disciples, if ye have love one to another.' The writer is fond of using two or more synonymous, or almost synonymous words ; v. p. 116, l. 17 note.

PAGE **109,** l. 4. *perseverance :* a technical term, especially in the form 'final perseverance ' for ' the preservation of the state of grace till the end of life' (*Cath. Enc.*), based on Matt. x. 22, 'He that endureth (or persevereth, Vulg. *Perseveraverit*) to the end shall be saved.'

l. 17. *police*: 'stationarius miles'; these were much like our police; in Rome they were under the command of the prefect of the city (v. p. 48, l. 4. note), in the provinces of the governor, and made reports to him of any disturbances, &c., and carried out his orders.

l. 33. *perfect*: Lat. 'immaculato'. The writer goes in front, who, though questioned, escaped martyrdom (v. Introd.); Marian and James, the future martyrs who should go before him to heaven, follow; but the order is 'perfect', because it conforms with our Lord's words (Matt. xix. 30, Mark x. 31), 'Many that are first shall be last, and the last first,' and suits the humility of the martyrs. The common reading is 'immutato', *unchanged*, but this does not accord with 'strangely' (' miro modo.')

PAGE 110, l. 13. *Decian persecution*: A.D. 250–1.

l. 16. *a reader*. The Second Edict of Valerian (v. Introd., p. 105) in July A.D. 258, punished with death, among the clergy, only bishops, priests, and deacons. Hence Marian who belonged to the lower order of Readers (v. p. 102, l. 19, note) was exempt. The authorities, however, thought he belonged to one of the higher orders and was concealing it, and so tortured him to make him confess.

l. 24. *his thumbs*. In Gallonius *de SS. Mart. cruciatibus* there is a picture of a martyr hanging tied up by the thumbs, with uneven weights attached to his feet (fig. iii. A, p. 23).

l. 31. *temple of God . . . joint heir with Christ*: cf. 1 Cor. vi. 19, 'Your body is the temple of the Holy Ghost,' &c.; Rom. viii. 17, 'Heirs of God, and joint-heirs with Christ; if so be that we suffer with Him, that we may be also glorified together.'

l. 32. *racked his sides*: lit. 'shook' or 'struck' his sides; it would naturally refer to beating, but there is no mention of that.

l. 34. *grew in body*. Under this and similar forms of torture, such as the 'horse', the limbs were actually lengthened; v. Sen. *ep.* lxvii. 'eculeo longior factus'; Sil. Ital. *Punica*, i. 177, 'Creverunt artus '; Prud. *Peristeph., hymn.* x. 109–10.

PAGE 111, l. 21. *scaffold*: 'catasta', gen. a raised platform on which slaves were sold; sometimes, as here, on which martyrs were tortured (cf. *Mart. Perp.*, p. 81, l. 35.)

l. 30. *Cyprian*: the famous Bishop of Carthage, martyred September 14, A.D. 258, nearly eight months previously (v. p. 93).

PAGE 112, l. 25. *a robe ungirt*: 'discincta,' a robe open in front, something like a B.A. or M.A. gown (cf. *Mart. Perp.*, ch. x.).

PAGE 113, l. 14. *double strictness*: 'gemina superpositione';

'superpositio' is an *addition* to an ordinary or stated fast, e. g. if instead of having *one* full meal, as usual, the penitent should have *nothing to eat*. A 'double addition', which is spoken of here, meant usually abstinence from drink as well as food.

PAGE 114, l. 20. *record :* 'elogio', a technical word for a judicial statement, containing an abstract of the charges, evidence for and against a prisoner.

l. 33. *again :* because they had been taken to the prison on their arrival, had left it for the examination by the governor, and had now returned to it.

Lambesa : an important city in Numidia, where an entire legion was quartered, 84 miles from Cirta.

PAGE 115, l. 14. *campaigns :* 'sacramenta' ; here the word seems to be used in a military sense ; sacramentum is the *military oath*, and so *military service*, and in the plural *campaigns*, cf. p. 123, l. 20, and note.

l. 32. *Love-feast :* the ἀγάπη, or Love-feast of the early Christians, at first combined with Holy Communion, 1 Cor. xi. 21 foll., cf. *Mart. Perp.*, p. 89, l. 1, and note.

PAGE 116, l. 17. *blood etc. :* 'cruorem . . . sanguinis', lit. 'gore of blood'. Sign. F. de' Cavalieri, *Stud. e test.*, iii, p. 40 (1900), notes that the African writers are fond of using a substantive followed by a genitive of the same meaning, e. g. Cyprian uses 'venenorum virus, lapsus ruinae, certaminis praelium', and of synonyms generally, 'dispositas agminum series per ordinem dirigebat, stragem corporum cumulus acervaret, niveo colore candentes,' in ch. xii. The Elizabethan writers, oddly enough, had a similar taste : Scott laughs at it in the person of Sir Piercie Shafton in *The Monastery*, e. g. ch. xv, 'The heat and warmth of the eye of day ', ' Strife, wrath, and all ireful passions', and it appears in our Book of Common Prayer, e. g. ' I pray and beseech you ', ' when we assemble and meet together '.

l. 19. *baptized . . . washed*. Martyrdom was regarded as equivalent to baptism, and was known as the ' Baptism of Blood ' ; v. *Mart. Perp.*, chs. xviii, xxi.

PAGE 117, l. 7. *clad in white :* cf. Rev. xix. 14, ' And the armies which were in heaven followed Him upon white horses, clothed in fine linen, white and clean.' They follow Him who was ' clothed with a vesture dipped in blood : and His name is called the Word of God.'

l. 16. *flies :* ' cynomiae,' Gr. κυνόμυια, variously regarded as the ' dogfly ', or, as Jerome, *Ep*. cvi. 86, prefers, flies generally (' omne muscarum genus ') ; indeed, he would write it κοινόμυια. It is used by the Old Latin translation of the Old Testament for the fourth plague of Egypt, Exod. viii. 21, and by the Vulgate in Ps. lxxviii. (lxxvii) 45, cv. (civ) 31, both in reference to the same plague.

For S. Marian's prophecy compare Rev. xv and xvi, esp. xv. 1, 'And I saw another sign in heaven . . . seven angels having the seven last plagues.' It was fulfilled (*Hist. Aug.* xxiii. 1 and 5), in the reign of Gallienus, Valerian's successor, by the civil wars (there were nineteen pretenders to the throne), barbarian inroads, inundations, earthquakes, and a plague, extending over the whole Roman world, which had begun in A.D. 250 and lasted till 265. In this reign Christianity became a ' religio licita ', i. e. permitted by the law.

l. 24. The mother of seven sons, all of whom were tortured and killed before her eyes for refusing to eat swine's flesh and give up their religion in the time of Antiochus Epiphanes (175–164 B.C.) ; 2 Macc. vii, esp. v. 20, ' But above all was the mother marvellous and worthy of honourable memory ; for when she looked on seven sons perishing within the space of one day, she bare the sight with a good courage for the hopes that she had set on the Lord.'

X. MARTYRDOM OF S. MARINUS

PAGE 119, l. 4. Caesarea Stratonis, on the coast, the seat of the Roman government in Palestine ; cf. Acts xxiii. 23, &c.

l. 8. The ' vine-switch ' was distinctive of the centurion, it was a mark of his power of inflicting corporal punishment.

PAGE 120, l. 1. Theotecnus was made Bishop of Caesarea in Palestine *c*. A. D. 260. Eusebius tells us (*Eccl. Hist.* vii. 14) that he was a disciple of Origen.

l. 7. The Evangeliarium or Book of the Gospels was the most venerated, and when possible most splendidly decorated, of all the Liturgical Books. It was placed in some conspicuous place in the Church, or even on the Altar. It was often enthroned at the beginning of Councils, as at Chalcedon, and was deposited in the Courts of Justice. There was another form, known as Evangelistarium, which contained only the Gospels read in the Liturgy, but this was rarely found till later. Note that S. Marinus, though a layman, has been admitted on this solemn occasion into the Sanctuary.

l. 18. *perfected :* cf. Luke xiii. 32, ' And the third day I shall be perfected ', and *Letter of the Churches of Vienne and Lyons*, ii. 3.

XI. ACTS OF S. MARCELLUS

PAGE 121, l. 1. *Tingis :* an ancient city on the north coast of Mauretania, capital of the Province of Mauretania, or Tingitana, now Tangier.

l. 2. *birthday of the Emperor :* or possibly the anniversary of his succession to the Empire, which was celebrated every fifth year.   The Emperor meant is Maximian (Herculius), who had charge of the West.

l. 6. A soldier wore two belts : (1) the 'cingulum' proper, which went round the waist, (2) the 'balteus', which went over the left shoulder and under the right arm, to which the sword was attached. 'Cingulum', however, was used as a generic term for both, and the 'balteus' is meant here (v. ch. ii. 'baltheum '), which was the distinctive mark of a soldier, of which he was stripped if degraded.   Hence the action of S. Marcellus here.

in front of the standards : because he had originally taken his oath of allegiance upon the standards.

Page **122**, l. 2. *vine-switch :* cf. *Mart. of S. Marinus*, ii and note. l. 4. *gods of wood and stone :* cf. Rev. ix. 20.

l. 11. *commander of the legion :* 'praesidi legionis ', the governor was head of the military as well as the civil organization of the province, hence he is here called 'commander of the legion '.   He held no military rank, and ' praeses ' is not a military term.

l. 13. *sitting in council :* 'residens in consistorio ', or ' in the council-chamber ', in any case not alone, but with assessors.

l. 15. *Asta :* 'Astasianis ', i. e. from Asta Regia, a city in the Province of Baetica in Southern Spain, near Cadiz, according to the Bollandist Acta SS. for October 30.

l. 27. *Emperors and Caesar :* Emperors Diocletian and Maximian, Caesar (in the West) Constantius, (Galerius was Caesar in the East).

l. 29. *Deputy for the Prefects of the Guard.*   There were at this time three or four Prefecti Praetorio, whose power was second only to that of the Emperor.   Under Augustus commanders of the Emperor's bodyguard, they now had the superintendence of all departments of the State, and had also a court in which they decided cases.

l. 30. 'Prosequente Caecilio acta officialia.'   This seems to be a note giving the name of the shorthand writer (v. p. 125, l. 4, note), who took down the proceedings in the court of Anastasius.   There was an official, 'ab actis ', who served as secretary to the Prefect of the Guard, and this might be the meaning here.   But the word ' prosequente ' 'following' 'keeping up with' the proceedings seems to make the translation in the text almost certain.

Page **123**, l. 17. *of the first class.*   The ' centuriones ordinarii ' were according to Mommsen, the three leading centurions in the first cohort of the three divisions of the legion, Pilani, Principes, and Hastati, known as Primipilus, Princeps Prior, and Hastatus Prior, who ranked next after the Tribune, or Colonel, of the legion.

l. 20. *signs of your allegiance :* 'sacramenta ' ;   in the singular it means *the military oath,* and so *allegiance* (as in chs. ii and v) : in the plural here it seems to mean the symbols of allegiance, the vine-switch and belt.

l. 35. *put on record :* ' deposuit ' ; this must be used almost in the modern sense of ' depose ', give ' evidence ', though I can find no example of the use either in Forcellini or Ducange.

XII. PASSION OF S. CASSIAN

PAGE **125**, l. 1. The MS. has here by mistake Aurelianus Auricu-lanus.

l. 4. *shorthand-writer :* ' exceptor ', also called ' notarius ' (which had a wider meaning). A system of shorthand seems to have been invented by Tiro, Cicero's secretary. It was used, as here, in the courts (cf. *Acts of S. Marcellus,* ch. ii), and extensively by the Christians to take down sermons, the proceedings of Councils (v. Augustine, *Ep.* 141) &c. It is to these ' exceptores ' that we probably owe many of the Acts (v. Le Blant, *Actes des Martyrs,* p. 10 foll., and my Gen. Introd., p. 15).

l. 6. For Asta and Tingis see notes to the *Acts of S. Marcellus.*

l. 17. *vowed with an imprecation :* lit. ' calling them to witness his curse on himself ', i. e. he prayed that he might be accursed if he went on.

l. 18. *pen :* ' graphium ', or ' stilus ', a pencil used for writing on waxed tablets, sharpened to a point at one end for scratching the characters on the wax, while the other end being flat and circular served to render the surface of the tablets smooth again, and so to obliterate what had been written (Smith's *Dict. of Gr. and Rom. Antiq.*).

l. 19. *note-book :* ' codicem ', wooden tablets bound together and lined with a coat of wax for the purpose of writing ; the word denotes also a book of parchment or paper (ib.).

PAGE **126**, l. 4. *obtained his desire :* adopting for the MS. reading, which is corrupt, Ruinart's conjecture, ' Marcellus beatissimus desideratum finem (or similar word) obtinuit.'

XIII. PASSION OF S. PROCOPIUS

PAGE **128**, ll. 4–6. *An example* . . . *discourses :* I have adopted Delehaye's translation here (*Legends of the Saints,* Eng. trans., p. 127), the sentence being corrupt (' Clementiae autem et mansuetudinis, tanquam ceteris inferior, documentum sui praebebat verbi copiam ').

l. 7. *of things without :* i. e. of profane literature.

l. 8. *Aelia :* the name given by the Emperor Hadrian to Jerusalem, which he restored ; the full name is Aelia Capitolina.

l. 9. *Scythopolis :* originally Bethsan, east of the Plain of Esdraelon, not far from the Jordan.

l. 11. *Reader :* 'lector', one of the four minor orders both in East and West, first mentioned in the middle of the 2nd century. During the early centuries all the lessons in the Liturgy, including the Epistle and Gospel were read by them (cf. p. 102, l. 19, p. 110, l. 16).

l. 12. *he cast out devils :* 'adversus daemones . . . consummans'. 'Consummo' sometimes means *to consecrate,* and so here it appears to mean 'restoring to holiness'. Exorcists were constituted as the third of the four minor orders of the Western Church about the middle of the third century. There is no such order in the Eastern Church.

l. 14. Caesarea Stratonis, the seat of Roman government in Palestine, on the sea-coast ; cf. Acts xxiii. 23, &c.

l. 23. *the Emperors :* Diocletian and Maximian.

l. 24. Homer, *Iliad,* ii. 204 :

οὐκ ἀγαθὸν πολυκοιρανίη· εἷς κοίρανος ἔστω
εἷς βασιλεύς (lit. *Let there be* one Lord, &c.).

l. 31. Desius, or Daesius, is the eighth month (out of 12) in the Ephesian year, a variety of the Macedonian, which was introduced into the East in the track of Alexander's conquests. Eusebius, in his brief notice of the martyrdom of Procopius in *Mart. Pal.* ch. i also gives the 7th of Daesius as the date, but explains it as the 7th day before the Ides of June, i. e. June 7th, which is correct according to the usual view of the place of this month in the calendar. S. Procopius is actually celebrated both in E. and W. on July 8th. Cf. note on p. 41, l. 7.

l. 33. *first martyrdom :* i. e. in this persecution. SS. Priscus and others had suffered at Caesarea under Valerian ; v. Eus. *Hist. Eccl.* vii. 12.

INDEX

OF SUBJECT MATTER

INDEX

OF NAMES AND PLACES

BIBLICAL QUOTATIONS
AND ALLUSIONS IN THESE ACTS

The references are to the page and line of the text. The words of the quotation will often be found in the Notes.

PRINTED IN ENGLAND AT THE
UNIVERSITY PRESS, OXFORD
BY JOHN JOHNSON
PRINTER TO THE UNIVERSITY

Date